WEST GLAMORGAN VILLAGES

Geoffrey Davies

SIGMA Leisure

Published by Sigma Leisure - an imprint of
Sigma Press, Stobart House, Pontyclerc, Penybanc Road, Ammanford, Carmarthenshire SA18 3HP.

British Library Cataloguing in Publication Data
A CIP record for this book is available from the British Library.

ISBN: 978-1-85058-982-2

Typesetting and Design by: Sigma Press, Ammanford.

Cover photograph: Merthyr Mawr © Geoffrey Davies

Printed by: TJ International Ltd, Padstow, Cornwall

Contents

Introduction

This book covers the villages of West Glamorgan in the new counties of Bridgend, Neath Port Talbot and the City and County of Swansea. Many villages have been swallowed up within the city of Swansea and these are not covered. There is always a problem in determining whether a community is a village or a town, especially when some villages have a much larger population than many towns.

The name Glamorgan is said to derive from Morgan, the son of King Arthur who ruled the county as king and established his court at Margam after the Saxons made Caerleon unsafe. It became known as Gwlad Morgan or Morgan's country.

In 1093 the Norman, Robert Fitzhamon seized Glamorgan and allocated the lands among his knights who established castles through the county. The descendants of some of these knights continued to play an important role in the life of the county for hundreds of years. The Normans brought with them stone churches and the concept of the monastic estate. The abbeys of Neath and Margam were granted vast areas of land which the monks used for agriculture and industry. Henry I introduced a large Flemish population to Wales in the 12th century, principally to South Pembrokeshire and Swansea and the Gower where there also came Anglo-Saxons from Somerset. While we use the term Norman, the Welsh at the time referred to the invaders as French. Sabine Baring-Gould, as late as the 19th century, observes "dialect in both (Pembrokeshire and Gower) is the same, and both are non-Welsh, and, indeed, a Gower man will not marry a Welsh woman. The Gower folk are thought to derive their pronunciation of adjectives ending in 'ous' like the French 'euse' from their contact with the Norman invaders and other Frenchmen settled in the peninsula."

The area covered by this book stretches from the Ogmore Valley in the east to the Gower and the River Loughor in the west. To the south is the Bristol Channel and the north the Brecon Beacons. The valleys of the Ogmore, Garw, Llynfi and Afan were little developed until the 19th century, with just a few hilltop villages. The much larger Vale of Neath became the site of large estates and one of the early tourist areas for travellers in search of the 'picturesque'. Roscoe describes the Vale of Neath : "enriched in effect by the many-coloured autumnal hues and the soft touches of the year's decline, it was in a peculiar degree both interesting and delightful. The vale exhibits several long reaches of quiet rural beauty, enclosed by two ranges of hills which run the whole extent, with occasional high rocks, feathered for the most part with forest foliage, and rearing above all their high and weather-beaten heads. Near the centre of the vale is the Melincourt Falls, a beautiful cascade, surrounded by romantic scenery."

Within the area are two rivers and a brook named Clydach, one flowing into the Tawe at Clydach, another into the Nedd or Neath River at Neath Abbey, while the Clydach Brook meets the Neath at Resolven. There are also two rivers named Dulais, with one joining the River Loughor at Pontardulais and the other the Neath at Aberdulais.

Much of the coastal strip between the Ogmore and Tawe estuaries is sand dune, one of the largest in Europe. The old castle and borough of Kenfig lie under the sand. Between the sand and the mountains lies an area with attractive old villages. West of Swansea lies the Gower with its fabulous coastline, castles and old villages.

The area saw amazing changes in the 19th century. The population of Glamorgan increased by 1,217% between 1811 and 1911 as the coal industry took off. In comparison, the next fifty years saw an increase of less than 10%. Villages sprang up overnight in previously deserted valleys. In 1911 there were 150,000 miners in the county. By 1984 there were just 21,500 in the whole of the South Wales area. This has meant many villages losing their *raison d'etre* and we are still in a time of transition as new employment opportunities are sought and a change from mining and heavy industry to modern manufacturing, technological and service industries and tourism develops.

Gradually, nature is reclaiming its own and the valleys are returning to some semblance of their former beauty. The evidence of the Industrial Age is disappearing in the same way as the Stone, Bronze and Iron Ages disappeared.

The villages have seen changes in social attitudes and behaviour. Perhaps the most striking change is the decline in religion with churches and chapels closing. Pubs too have closed as economic forces, drink driving and changing habits come into play. Yet not all villages have seen these effects. Some have retained all their churches, chapels and pubs.

English is the predominant language in the area, though Welsh is still spoken as a first language in some areas. Throughout the book I have tried to offer an explanation of the name of each village. Some prefixes and suffixes are common. 'Llan' referred to the ground on which a church is built, traditionally circular, though the term is now used for church and is usually followed by its dedication. 'Aber' refers to the mouth of the river. 'Cwm' is valley with 'Glyn' the equivalent of Glen and 'Dyffryn', Vale. 'Blaen' refers to the source of a river. A number of villages with English names carry the suffix 'ton', meaning a dwelling place or town. So Reynoldston is Reynold's dwelling place or town. The Welsh equivalent is the prefix 'tre'.

Spelling in both English and Welsh was not standardized until the latter part of the 19th century. Where quotations from old texts are used, the original spelling has been retained. In Welsh the first letter of a word can mutate if it follows another word. For example 'bach' meaning little becomes 'fach' in Felinfach meaning little mill.

While there are a number of guttural sounds in Welsh, phonetically, the language is consistent with the emphasis placed on the penultimate syllable of a word. The exception is marked by a circumflex as in 'â' which has the effect of lengthening the vowel sound and changing the emphasis to the final syllable.

Villages of West Glamorgan

Abercregan

Abercregan is a former mining village on the northern side of the River Afan west of the village of Cymer. The Corrwg Vale Colliery was a small mine employing just 82 men in 1896. The company was formally dissolved in 1928. The village has declined in size, losing its chapel, hotel, Miners Welfare Hall and school as well as the majority of its housing. The South Wales Mineral Railway ran through the village and there was a tramway from Troed Y Rhiw where stone was quarried. Nearer the village are the Abercregan Grottos, caves the result of quarrying which are now fenced off.

Above the village to the north-west are a number of cairns thought to be Bronze Age in an area now dominated by wind turbines.

Aberdulais

Aberdulais is a village in the Neath valley at the confluence of the Neath and Dulais rivers. It was formerly known as Dylas.

The village is rich in industrial history with the Dulais providing power for various industries over the years on a site now in the care of the National Trust. The junction of the Neath and Tennant Canal systems is in the village.

The site took advantage of the River Dulais being squeezed into a gorge and producing a waterfall. It was the subject of a watercolour by J. W. M. Turner in 1796, which is now in the possession of the National Library of Wales. A copper smelting works was established here in the 16th century and the site was subsequently used as a corn mill, ironworks and tinplate works. The tinplate works were established in 1830 and manufacturing continued until 1939 on the lower part of the complex having been abandoned on the upper part in 1890. The waterwheel has been reconstructed and is now used to produce electricity for the site with the surplus being fed into the National Grid. It is the largest electricity generating waterwheel in Europe. The

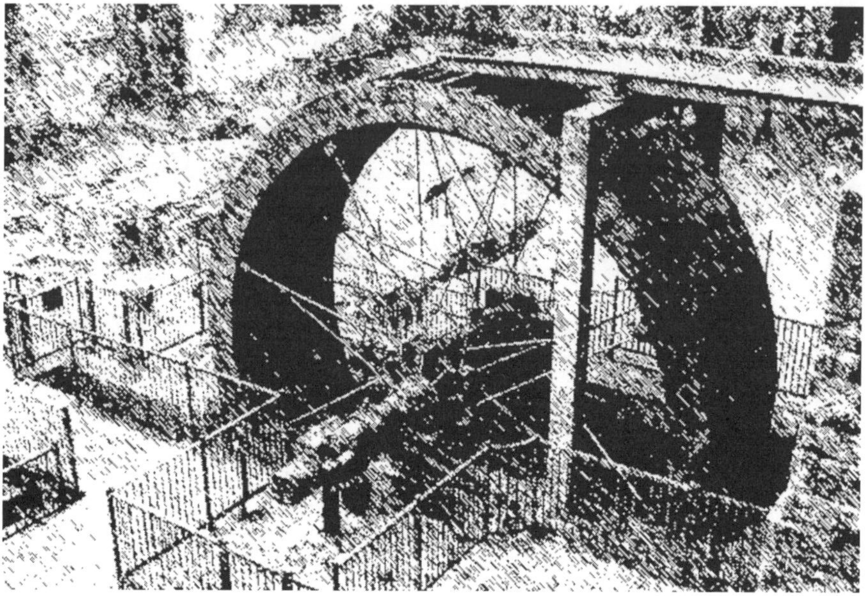

The waterwheel at Aberdulais

site is open daily from March to October and at weekends November to the end of February.

The Neath valley below the falls is now dominated by the Heads of the Valleys dual carriageway, but as the River Neath travels through the valley it is crossed by the Aberdulais Aqueduct constructed in 1823 to carry the Tennant Canal. The Neath Canal built in 1795 follows a line to the east of the river and the Tennant Canal provides a link to Swansea Docks. There is a working lock and the old canal wharf.

Aberdulais was served by two rail lines, the one from Neath to Aberdare and the other Neath to Brecon. Neither track reaches its final destination today and there is no passenger service, though both are still operational for goods trains.

The village of Aberdulais has a mix of housing and there is a golf course and hotel, though the latter appeared closed at the time of writing.

Aberdulais Wesleyan Methodist Chapel was built in 1902 alongside the canal. It is no longer in use as a chapel.

Aberdulais Baptist Chapel was built in 1856, rebuilt in 1863 and 1899. Situated opposite the Dulais Rock Hotel, it was demolished for the dual carriageway.

Seion Calvinistic Methodist Chapel was built in 1839 and rebuilt in 1860. Situated above the A4109 near its junction with Fforest Hill it is of the long wall double entry style and overlooks the valley.

Abergarwed

Abergarwed is a former coal mining village in the Vale of Neath on the north-western side of the river near Resolven. Today the village is well maintained with attractive views across the valley and some new housing.

The Ynysarwed Collieries operated two mines, one situated to the west of the village the other to the east and operated intermittently between 1847 and 1955. There were two small mines to the east of the Garwed Brook, now hidden in scrub with an inclined tramway.

There are two locks below the village on the Neath Canal.

Old maps show Ebenezer Congregational Chapel at the south-western end of the village, but it is no longer in existence.

Abergwynfi and Blaengwynfi
Mouth of the Gwynfi and Source of the Gwynfi

Situated high in the Afan valley on the road from Treherbert to Aberavon, the twin villages of Aber and Blaen Gwynfi owe their existence to the Avon or Afan colliery begun in 1877 by Sir Daniel Gooch of the Great Western Railway (GWR). The terraces of houses with their chapels followed, as did the railways. First the Abergwynfi to Maesteg line using a tunnel from Cymer to Caerau in the Llynfi Valley was opened by the GWR in 1886. The line from Blaengwynfi to Treherbert and Aberavon was built by the Rhondda and Swansea Bay Railway in 1890, eventually reaching Swansea Riverside in 1894. The tunnel from Blaengwynfi to Treherbert is 3,443 yards long and the longest rail tunnel in Wales. As well as coal trains there was a regular passenger service. Each railway company had its own station, though the Rhondda and Swansea Bay Railway was taken over by GWR in

1907. The tunnel is celebrated in the Tunnel Hotel in Gwynfi Street Blaengwynfi. The line from Treherbert was never profitable because the incline was too great to allow fully loaded trains and both lines fell to the Beeching axe in the 1960s.

The Avon Colliery had a chequered history. In 1896 there were 559 men employed producing steam coal and the numbers increased to 907 in 1908, but in 1910 the pit was mothballed with just 30 maintenance staff. The Ocean Coal Company took over in 1911 and production resumed in 1915. Employment reached a post war peak in 1923 with 672 men but by 1945 there were just 113 working at the colliery which eventually closed in 1969.

St Gabriel's Church was built in the early 1890s to plans by G. E. Halliday. Left derelict for many years it has now been converted to accommodation with the bellcote removed.

There were a number of chapels in the villages, mainly built in the 1890s, including Tabor Independent, Caersalem Baptist, now disused, Villiers Road Presbyterian, Soar Independent Chapel in Mary Street, built in 1907 but now used as a store and Bethel Baptist Jersey Road Chapel, converted to a dwelling.

There are a number of shops in Jersey Road and Commercial Street. Jersey Road also has the 1901 Abergwynfi and Blaengwynfi Workmen's Hall Institute and Library. Still in use as a library and social club, the hall functioned for many years as a cinema, at one time seating 800, though later reduced to 448.

Part of the old colliery is now used by Alchemy Technologies Ltd.

There is a futuristic Primary School built in 2009.

Today the villages are in the Afan Forest Park and gradually the signs of mining are giving way to forestry. The railway tracks to the south form part of a cycle way and the area is being developed for mountain biking.

Aberkenfig

This is village where I grew up in the 1950s and early 1960s. I remember a busy village with its two cinemas, two butchers, two fruiterers, two fish and chip shops, clothes shops, the Cooperative stores, Perkins the bakers and grocery store, the bike and toy shop, chemists, three pubs, and the churches and chapels. The police station under Sergeant Barrel was manned and two policemen would patrol at 11 o'clock each night, trying doors to ensure they were locked.

The changes reflect our society. The cinemas are no longer, the Cinema, a corrugated iron building on Bridgend Road has disappeared completely while the Lyric is now the Aberkenfig Bible Church. The pubs remain, but Ebenezer Chapel is now a furniture store, Carey is closed and boarded up, while Trinity, just off the square, was demolished one Sunday morning in the 1960s. Beulah, the corrugated iron chapel, appears to be flourishing. The food stores have disappeared, to be replaced by takeaway restaurants, a Private Shop and hairdressers. The owners of the bike and toy shop switched to television and electrical items long ago.

Aberkenfig developed as a village in the 19th century, when the Parc Slip drift coal mine was expanded. Some mining had been carried on in the area from the early 16th century when the Abbot of Margam Abbey leased the land at Cwm Ffos, to the west of the present village for mining. Parc Slip was developed in 1864 by the Ogmore Coal and Iron Company and by 1899 had been taken over by North's Navigation Company. The coal produced was house and gas coal. On August 26th, 1892 at 8.20 in the morning, an explosion thought to have been caused by a broken glass in a Davy Lamp, led to the death of 110 men and boys. Work resumed and in 1896 the mine employed 268 men. Park Slip closed in 1904. The site was worked for opencast mining in the 1960s and has since been reclaimed as a nature reserve and there is a memorial stone. There were other mines in the area, including the Cribwr Colliery with its coke ovens, situated to north of Meadow Street.

By the 1950s Aberkenfig had no large industry with work provided in the rail yards of Tondu, the National Coal Board regional offices at Tondu, the Tondu Brickworks and further afield at the giant Margam Abbey steelworks and the growing industrial estate at Bridgend.

The local infants' schools were at Tondu and Pandy and the Tondu Infants School, together with Tondu Primary School were merged in a new school at the western end of West Street and Meadow Street. Pandy takes its name from a woollen mill or pandy mill while there was another woollen mill at the southern end of the village.

Aberkenfig takes its name from the diminutive Nant Cynffig which joins the Ogmore River here. The slightly larger Afon Cynffig flows past Kenfig Hill.

The Church of St John the Divine was built as a chapel of ease to the parish of Newcastle Higher in 1866-68 to plans by John Prichard of London and Llandaff. It was a large church and the original plans showed the intention of adding both south and north transepts at a later stage. The south transept was duly built and a vestry added in place of the north transept. St John's subsequently became a parish in its own right in 1923, taking in the church of Coytrahen. It was subsequently merged with Pen-y-fai.

Across the River Ogmore sits the older church of Llansantffraid, in the parish of St Brides Minor. A 13th century church it has a nave, chancel and western bellcote with an additional northern aisle. It is now cut off from Aberkenfig by a new road and is accessible on foot or bicycle from the village or by car from Sarn along Heol Persondy.

One of the characters of post war Aberkenfig was Eric Beardshaw, who preferred to be known as Eric Shaw. Educated at Marlborough College, Eric spent time in the United States before becoming a gentleman's hairdresser in the village. A gifted pianist he acted as an impresario, making the most of his American accent when putting on concerts at Bridgend's Town Hall, before it was demolished. Eric's greatest moment came when he introduced a young singer on Hughie Green's *Opportunity Knocks.*

Alltwen *White Wooded Slope*

Alltwen is a village built on the side of a hill south of Pontardawe.

The church of St John The Baptist was built in 1886 above Dyffryn Road. Because of the difficulty in providing disabled access it was closed in 2005 and has since been converted to private accommodation, with glass set into the ridge of the roof. The bellcote has been retained. Church services are now held in the 1893 former church school and reading room built by Mrs Gwyn, wife of Howel Gwyn M.P. of Dyffryn and named the Gwyn Hall in her honour. The building has been modified and extended to become the new St John the Baptist Church.

Next to the new church is Alltwen Independent Chapel, built in 1757, and rebuilt three times, the last in 1886.

The village saw a rapid post war expansion in the 20th century. It retains the Butchers Arms though the Gwyn Arms has closed and the Celtic Lodge was for sale at the time of writing. There is no post office, but there is a primary school.

The main industry for the village in the past was quarrying with disused quarries in the area of Bryn Llewellyn.

Baglan

Baglan takes its name from St Baglan to whom the original church was designated. Lewis, in 1831, described the village as "delightfully situated in the midst of rich and beautifully diversified scenery, bounded on one side by mountains whose acclivities are thickly wooded, and commanding over the lower grounds a magnificent view of Swansea bay. The beauty of its situation, and the local advantages it possesses, has made it a favourite place of residence; and within its limits, in addition to the neat cottages which are profusely scattered over its surface, is a greater number of gentlemen's seats than is usually to be found in a single parish. The village has an air of rural simplicity, and a prepossessing appearance of cheerfulness and tranquillity. The soil is of different kinds, part being meadow and grazing land of good quality, and some tolerably good arable land; but the greater portion of the parish consists of mountainous ground, affording merely pasturage for sheep, and on the side next the sea are extensive banks and plains of sand. There are several veins of coal of a good bituminous quality, of which some are worked; and a considerable quantity of fine clay is obtained, part of which is used in the manufacture of earthenware, and part conveyed to the different copper-works in the neighbourhood; together with some iron-ore, which is smelted at the Neath Abbey iron-works. A creek, called Baglan Pill, which falls into the Neath a little below Briton Ferry, affords a facility for conveying the produce of the mines, and other commodities, in craft of from twenty to thirty tons' burthen. The great South Wales railway, also, will pass near Baglan. The church, dedicated to St. Baglan, is a neat and appropriate building, and the churchyard is shaded with yew-trees of luxuriant growth. In 1844 a National school for boys and girls was established at Pant-y-Swan. ... Of the gentlemen's seats with which the parish is adorned, the principal are, Baglan House, the residence of Howel Gwyn, Esq., once the residence of the Rev. William Thomas, by whom it was built, the friend of Mason and Gray, who were his occasional visiters; Baglan Hall, the seat of Griffith Llewellyn, Esq."

Baglan today is almost unrecognizable from this description. Baglan House dating from 1760 was demolished in 1961 to make way for housing and the older Baglan Hall dating from the 16th century was demolished in 1958 to create a park. A dual carriageway, the M4 Motorway and the railway line all pass between Baglan and the sea. St Baglan's Church is now a shell, having burnt down in 1954. It had already been replaced in 1882 by St Catherine's Church, designed by John Prichard. St Catherine's is a cruciform church with a crossing tower topped by a spire. The interior is highly decorated in the late Victorian tradition. The church of St Baglan was Norman, but built on the site of a Celtic church as evidenced by the 9th century incised cross now housed in the vestry of St Catherine's. The old church school stands in Old Road.

The greatest change however has been in the vast increase in housing which took place in the latter part of the 20th century. The area of Baglan Moors to the south of the M4, once deserted, has been consumed by supermarkets, industrial units and the Neath Port Talbot Hospital.

There are two inns in the village, the Bagle Brook which is a Beefeater pub with Premier Inn adjoining and the Tyn y Twr Tavern in St Illtyd's Close. There is a small retail area with mini supermarket, bakery and hairdressers.

Baglan has two primary schools, Blaenbaglan and Baglan.

There was limited coal mining in the village and Park Colliery stood where Willow Way now runs. It had closed by 1900.

East of St Baglan's Church once stood Plas Baglan, a Welsh built castle or fortified mansion built in the late 12th century and occupied until the 17th century. The tower of Plas Baglan is alluded to in the name of the Tyn y Twr Tavern. The scant foundations are overgrown.

It was recorded that in 1756 Christopher Turberville of Aberavon, a labourer, together with another man were charged that "at the parish of Baglan, with force and arms of and from one James Carson (and another person) did demand money with divers menaces, using these Welsh words: "Sefwch, God dammoch chwi, efe ceiswch arian chwi"" translated as: "Stand, God damn you, I want your money!" The accused were convicted of highway robbery.

Banwen *White Peak*

Banwen is a small hamlet on the mountain between the Neath and Swansea valleys. Built on the line of the Roman Road, Sarn Helen, it consists of a single street of terraced houses though a few new houses have been added as has the Jehovah's Witness Kingdom Hall.

The housing was built along with Maesmarchog Colliery in 1845 though mining had started a century earlier. The colliery later became Onllwyn No. 3, but was normally referred to as Banwen. It was in its day a large drift mine but closed in 1962. Since the closure of the mine there has been extensive opencast mining to the south of the village and the area has now developed into the Walters Arena Motorsports Complex which has 65 miles of road for rallying and is used as part of the World Rally Championship Wales GB course.

To the north of the village, following the line of Sarn Helen which runs from Neath to Brecon, is a Roman Marching Camp and a Roman Fort.

Banwen lays claim to being the birthplace of St Patrick and a stone commemorating the fact has been erected on Roman Road. Patrick himself wrote that he was the son of deacon Calpurnius, son of the late Potitus, a presbyter, of the settlement of Bannaven Taburniae. The old name of Banwen was Tafarn y Banwen. (Other versions split the Latin as Banna Venta Burniae and identify it as Ravenglass in Cumbria). The Tavern y Banwen was recorded in 1695 when the poet Dafydd Nicholas drank there. It closed in 1916 and was demolished in 1937.

In 1962 the Banwen Miners Hunt was formed, initially exclusively from members of the village. It has expanded over the years and celebrated its 50th anniversary in 2012. Since 1976 it has run an annual Point to Point race near Resolven.

A standing stone on Sarn Helen with the Latin inscription 'the tomb of Macaritinus, son of Beri' was removed to Lady Mackworth's garden grotto in Neath until a violent storm destroyed the grotto and now resides in Swansea Museum. Legend had it that fairies used to be seen around the stone riding horses. It was said that on the destruction of the grotto people heard fairy laughter. A replica stone has now been placed in the original location.

Birchgrove

Birchgrove today is a large commuter village with a population of 6,000. There is a mixture of housing, much built in the last 30 years. It is situated six miles north of Swansea, bordering the M4. It has a primary and comprehensive school, supermarket, The Crown Inn and The Bridge End Inn.

Birchgrove was a mining village, with the Birchgrove Colliery started in 1845 producing steam coal. The colliery was sited at the north end of the village between Heol Las and Birchgrove Road. A second shaft known as the Sisters Pit was opened half a mile to the north, while a further pit known as the Brothers was sunk in 1887 a quarter of a mile to the west of Birchgrove Colliery. Mining continued until 1932 employing up to 350 men.

Saron Chapel was built in 1871 Nazareth Calvinistic Methodist Chapel was built in 1876 and rebuilt in 1906, situated at the junction of Drumau Road and Birchgrove Road it was closed in 1992 and has been demolished. A bungalow now occupies the site.

St John's Church was built as a chapel of ease in the parish of Llansamlet in 1891. A small church, seating just 100, it has a west tower and porch but is otherwise a single cell construction with vestry. It is set in an acre of land with the church hall.

Bishopston

Bishopston or to give its Welsh name Llandeilo Ferwallt (Church of Teilo 'Ferwallt' translates as 'short hair') is an ancient village at the southern entrance to the Gower from Swansea. According to the Book of Llandaff the church was founded by Teilo in the 5th century with the stone church erected in the late 12th century. The church, which is built in a dell, no doubt originally to protect it from the view of sea borne marauders, is on a north-west to south-east axis, indicating the direction of sunrise on the Saint's day of February 9th when the sun is low in the sky. The roof was thatched until the 1830s. There was a restoration in the 1890s affecting the interior of the church but the Norman font remains. In the churchyard are the remains of a medieval cross.

It is thought that there was a 10th century bishop's palace in the village on land near the school.

South of the church in a field on Backington Farm are the remains of a small medieval chapel.

Bishopston has expanded considerably in the last 50 years and subsumed the hamlet of Pyle. It has its range of schools including Bishopston Comprehensive, consistently rated among the top ten comprehensives in England and Wales. House prices in this area are above average. There is a range of small shops and the Joiners Arms and The Valley inns.

To the south of the village are the beaches of Pwlldu Bay and Brandy Cove, both only accessible on foot. Further east is the popular Caswell Bay.

Blackmill

Blackmill is a village in the Ogmore valley five miles north of Bridgend. In the 19th century it had both a corn and woollen mill as well as a railway station. Apart from the mills, the main occupation was quarrying and farming. It is at the confluence of the Rivers Ogwr Fawr and Ogwr Fach and the junction of roads to Bridgend, Ogmore Vale and Gilfach Goch. It was also the junction of railways, giving the name to one of two pubs in the village, the Ogmore Junction. The other is the Fox and Hounds and both are on the square, together with a shop, post office café and service station.

The village has expanded with new housing and an industrial park in the last 40 years. The old railway is now a walking and cycling track.

Blackmill Wesleyan Methodist Chapel was built in 1885 but has been demolished and housing built on the site. It was originally a school for boys and girls. Paran Baptist Chapel was built in 1819 is Grade II Listed. It was altered or enlarged in 1859, 1889 and 1898 when a gallery was added.

All Saints Mission Church was built in 1915 but has been demolished. The village offers attractive walks through the valley.

Blaengarw

Blaengarw is a village at the northern end of the Garw valley, eight miles from Bridgend. The name refers to the source of the Garw or 'rough' river. The village sprang up in the last 20 years of the 19th century as coal mining came to the valley.

The slopes of the valley are littered with the evidence of trial mines and abandoned small scale workings. There were workings at Nant Hir with a tram road to Cwm Gelliwern where there was an engine shed and trial workings. Activity at both sites had ceased by 1919. The industrialization of the valley really started when the International Colliery was sunk in 1874 at Pwllcarn. At its peak in 1896 it employed 1,015 men and it continued in operation until 1968. The Darren Fawr Colliery opened in the 1880s and employed up to 246 men before closing in 1923. The Ffaldau Colliery was sunk in 1878 and was linked with the New Braichycymmer Colliery, also known as the Victoria Colliery. Ffaldau closed in 1985. The Ocean Colliery opened in 1883 and employed up to 750 men. In 1975 it linked underground with the Ffaldau Colliery and operated as a single unit until closure in 1985.The Glengarw Colliery was opened in the 1890s. At its peak it employed 662 men. It closed in 1959. Much of the evidence of the coal industry has disappeared though the spoil heaps can still be seen at the top of the valley, now greened over.

As is common in villages like Blaengarw the chapels soon followed the opening of the pits.

Bethania Baptist Chapel in Herbert Street was built in 1890 and rebuilt in 1912. Bethania is now Grade II Listed but is no longer in use and subject to vandalism. Nebo Independent Chapel in Katie Street was built in 1890 but has been demolished. Mount Zion Baptist Chapel in King Edward Street was built in 1900 and rebuilt in 1905. Tabernacle Calvinistic Methodist Chapel was built in 1891 in Katie Street. Trinity Methodist Chapel on The Strand was built in 1887 and rebuilt in 1903; the chapel has been demolished and a block of flats stands in its place.

St James Church was built in 1891 by the architects E. H. Bruton and E. J. Williams of Cardiff. It consisted of a nave, chancel with two small transepts, a southern porch and western bellcote. It has now been converted to a private dwelling.

Blaengarw Workingmen's Hall and Institute was built in 1893 and opened in 1894. The Hall contained a library and reading room, cinema and theatre, as well as meeting rooms. The building has been restored and is in use as an arts and community venue.

Other than local authority or association housing there has been little house building in the village in the last 100 years. There are a number of shops, a community centre, clubs and the Blaengarw Hotel. The surrounding area has the attractions of the hills, which are scattered with cairns. As well as rugby and football pitches there is a lake for fishing and a picnic and recreation area where the old railway sidings once stood. The railway track has been removed and is in use as a cycle way and footpath. The valley slopes are well wooded creating an attractive environment reminiscent of the early 19th century when sheep farming was the norm for the few farms in the area.

Blaengwrach and Cwm Gwrach

These villages are divided by the Nant Gwrach, but fall within the same community and Blaengwrach Primary School lies in Cwmgwrach.

Former mining and iron industry villages, they lie across the River Neath from Glyn Neath.

Lewis described Blaengwrach in 1831 with the following: "The village is situated near the head of the vale of Neath, which is here seen in all its varied and romantic beauty: the striking character of its scenery, abounding with luxuriant verdure, is heightened by contrast with the sterile brow of a lofty mountain, which towers above the neighbouring hills, and the rocky declivities of which are indented by numerous deep fissures, through which, after heavy rains, or rapid thaws, the waters rush down in impetuous torrents, exhibiting a scene of awful grandeur and sublimity. The river Gwrach, from which the village takes its name, swollen with the mountain streams that augment its waters, frequently overflows its banks, and inundates the adjacent meadows, which become one entire sheet of water. Ynislaes, an elegant cottage built by the Hon. Windham Henry Wyndham Quin, now Earl of Dunraven and Mountearl, and for some time his own residence, occupies a beautiful situation, commanding a delightful view of the rich vale of Neath, through its whole extent."

According to Lewis the chapelry of Blaengwrach was the birthplace of Dr Abraham Rees whose father was Lewis Rees, the pastor of the independent congregation. Abraham Rees revised the *Cyclopædia of Ephraim Chambers* before publishing his own *The New Cyclopædia, or Universal Dictionary of Arts and Sciences ... Biography, Geography, and History* in 1802, claimed to be the most extensive work ever completed by an individual. He was elected a Fellow of the Royal Society in 1786, but continued as a lecturer and independent minister in London where the octagonal meeting house in Jewin Street was built for him. He published a number of volumes of his sermons and assisted in compiling *A Collection of Hymns and Psalms* for use by independent congregations.

Today the villages still benefit from the magnificent scenery and are now largely commuter villages. There has been new housing and the villages retain a mini supermarket and post office, but the Dunraven Arms appears to have gone.

The Venallt Ironworks were established in around 1840 but lasted only until 1854. Situated on what is now the correctly spelt Wenallt Farm (there is no 'V' in Welsh), there are a number of features remaining including the blowing-house engine, part of the cast-house, the base of the stack and the furnace walls. To the west of the site is the Rackwood Coaling Plant with its rail lines down to Neath.

Coal mining started in the area around 1800 and an explosion at the local mine in 1820 killed five, including girls of six and twelve years of age. In 1898 Caerbryn and Empire Collieries sank a new pit into the old workings at the Empire Colliery. By 1918 it employed 360 men, increasing to 1,000 with the opening of two new shafts in the 1920s. In 1962 the National Coal Board started production from the Blaengwrach Mine. At its peak the mines were producing 4,400 tons a week, but by 1983 this had fallen to just 82 tons a week and the pits were closed.

Opencast mining in the form of the massive Selar Mine started above the village in 1997 with an output of between 8,000 and 10,000 tons per week. It occupies a site near the former Dunraven-Adare colliery which at one time was owned by the Williams family of Aberpergwm.

Cwmgwrach's Siloh Independent Chapel was built in 1862 and modified in 1892. In Blaengwrach, Calfaria Baptist Chapel was built in 1905 while a Unitarian Chapel was built in 1704 and rebuilt in 1830 about 150 yards south-east of the rugby pitch above the village. It was demolished in 1946.

St Mary's church in Blaengwrach was built as a chapel of ease to Glyncorrwg in 1704 (some give an earlier date). It was rebuilt in 1830, being transferred to the parish of Aberpergwm in 1950. In 2007 it saw a conversion to enable its use as a community hall as well as a church. Melin Clun-y-Bont was a 16th century corn mill situated on the River Neath close to the Rackwood Coal Plant. Originally the manor's mill, it survived into the 19th century.

The oldest monuments are on the mountain above the opencast mine. Adjoining the Coed Morgannwg Way are three cairns believed to date from the Bronze Age.

Bryn *Hill*

Bryn, or to give it its full name Bryn Troed y Garn (Hill at the Foot of the Cairn), is a former mining village in the hills between Maesteg and the Afan valley.

The area around the village was rich in outcrops of coal used by the farmers for heating and burning lime. Some mining was carried out by the monks of Margam Abbey, but it was not until the 19th century that large scale mining came to the village. The first mine opened in the 1840s and the population rose from 111 to 558 in ten years. By 1876 there were four mines in operation, Bryngurnos Colliery, Bryn Colliery, Drysiog with three levels and Bryntroedygarn with two levels. By 1900 all had closed or replaced by the Bryn Navigation Colliery which continued in production until 1964 employing up to 683 men. A railway was constructed to take coal to the copper works in the Afan valley and this was extended with the Cwm Cerwyn Tunnel in 1897 to link Port Talbot with Maesteg. This line also closed in 1964.

With the influx of people came the chapels. Jerusalem English Baptist Chapel was built in 1852 and rebuilt in 1885. Though now a private dwelling, the baptistry was enclosed by rails and had a well beneath the floorboards. Jerusalem is Grade II Listed as a well-preserved 19th century chapel with a fine gallery of a rare panelled design. Carmel Independent Chapel was built in 1846, rebuilt in 1860 and 1928. It had fallen into disuse by 1998.

Bryn Seion Welsh Calvinistic Methodist Chapel was built in 1856 and rebuilt in 1914. By 1984 it had fallen into disuse. St Tydfil's church was built in 1902 with a donation from Miss Emily Charlotte Talbot, who also donated the money for a vicarage and church hall. This church too was demolished in the 1990s and the land sold for housing. The proceeds were used to convert the church hall into the new St Tydfil's church.

Today the village has a new lease of life with new housing. The tips which littered the village have disappeared and the surrounding countryside provides a pleasant environment. There is a modern school, community centre and a post office. The Royal Oak Hotel stands at the entrance to the village travelling from Maesteg.

Brynaman *Aman Hill*

Brynaman or Brynamman is divided between Carmarthenshire and Neath Port Talbot. The boundary is the River Aman. Lower Brynaman lies in the old county of Glamorgan.

Originally the village was known as Y Gwter Fawr or the Big Gutter after the high pressure water methods of extracting coal had created a large gutter. The first mention of Brynamman was a house built in 1838 by John Jones, the second son of John Jones of Brynbrain, who had started the first mine in the village in the first decade of the 19th century. When the Swansea Vale Railway reached the village in 1864 the station was named Brynamman. The spelling changed to Brynaman when new rules on Welsh grammar were introduced ruling out the double 'M'.

George Borrow stayed at the Farmers Arms in Lower Brynaman in 1855. The pub which was built in 1823 was later rebuilt and became the Brynamman Hotel. It is now a private house. The New Farmers Arms is now Brynaman Rugby Club.

Much of what became known as Lower Brynaman is shown on the 1877 map as Glyn y beudy.

By 1900 the village was a major mining and industrial centre. The Gwter Fawr which ran through Lower Brynaman, entering the Aman near the Farmers Arms had all but disappeared by 1860, but there were collieries to the east of the village in the area which has since been subjected to opencast mining and landscaping. Tramways led to the Amman Iron Works, which had been established by John Jones but were enlarged after being taken over in 1847 by the Amman Iron Works company owned by Llewellyns. Two blast furnaces were added and in 1851 a forge. In 1868 the third furnace was added, known as Big Furnace and a tinplate works added across the river in Upper Brynaman in 1872. Part of the old iron works can be seen in what was the coal yard up river from the bridge.

Hermon Independent Chapel was built in 1905, Siloam Baptist Chapel was built in 1871 and altered in 1898, while Ebenezer Independent Chapel was built in 1882 and rebuilt in 1898. St Catherine's Church is situated in Upper Brynaman.

Today the village has a garage, post office and primary school. There is some modern housing but the Crown Hotel has closed. There are walks across the common and along the river.

Bryncethin *Dark Hill*

Bryncethin is a village three miles north of Bridgend.

Large deposits of clay and coal led to the purchase of Glassbrook Colliery in 1873 by the Barrow-in-Furness Hematite Steel Co. Mining had started in a small way in the village in the 1830s and the Glassbrook Colliery was started in 1870. The Barrow company also built a brickworks. The new colliery required a larger workforce and much of the housing in the village dates to this time. The Barrow Company had its base in Wigan, hence the Wigan Terrace name. The company pulled out in 1888 and French and Belgian companies tried to operate the mines. The colliery closed in 1915 to be reopened and finally closed in 1921. The brickworks were sold to Charles Jenkins and Son of Bridgend.

While the heart of the village has changed little over the last 50 years, the surrounding area has seen major changes. The removal of the railway bridge below the village has enabled a new road system and new housing developments. There are two general stores, a hairdressers and the Masons Arms Hotel. The Dunraven Hotel is closed.

Nazareth Baptist Chapel was built in 1887, Bethania Calvinistic Methodist Chapel was built in the early 20th century but has now been demolished, Peniel Independent Chapel was built in 1825 and rebuilt in 1888 but no longer in use as a chapel, while Halleluiah Wesleyan Methodist Chapel was built in the early 20th century in the Arts and Crafts style but is now used as a farmers' market.

Bryncoch *Red Hill*

Bryncoch is a commuter village bordering the A474 Neath to Pontardawe road. Between 1806 and 1929 there were a number of collieries in and around the village employing up to 2,000 men.

The River Clydach flows through the village and until 1860 powered a corn mill to the west of the village.

The village saw a rapid expansion during the 1960s with a number of large housing developments and has the reputation of having one of the highest average household incomes in the area.

The church of St Matthew was built on his Dyffryn estate by Howel Gwyn M.P. in 1871. The church has a nave, chancel, south tower and north porch.

Ainon Baptist Chapel was built in 1906 and the brick built Saron Independent Chapel in 1857.

The village retains three pubs, the Dyffryn Arms, the Lamb and Flag, and the Bryncoch Inn. There are two schools and the Ysgol Hendre special school.

Brynmenyn *Butter Hill*

Brynmenyn is a village between Tondu and Bryncethin, and developed in the early part of the 20th century. In 1900 there were just a few houses scattered around the junction of the Ogmore and Garw railway lines and Betharran Independent Chapel was built in 1809, rebuilt in 1859, and rebuilt again in 1925. The chapel is now a private dwelling. There is a Calvinistic Methodist Chapel in Bryn Road of the 20th century.

To the east of the village was the Abergarw Brewery, established in the late 19th century but disused by 1942. The site was previously occupied by a woollen mill which may have been a much earlier tucking or fulling mill. There was a millrace running from the weir on the River Ogmore which powered a corn mill as well as the woollen mill.

Ynysawdre Colliery was situated south-west of the village on what is now the site of the Archbishop Mcgrath Comprehensive School. It was started prior to 1875 and 50 coke ovens had been built on the site by 1890, though closed in 1900. The colliery which was later named the Adare Colliery closed in 1898. Later attempts to mine there were abandoned. There was also a colliery to the north of Abergarw which was short lived. There was a brickworks in the 1880s just north of the village alongside the Afon Garw.

The rail line to the Garw is still in place though marked as disused, with the level crossing gates remaining in situ next to the Fox and Hounds. The Ogmore track is now a cycle path and walkway. The line to Llanharan has been dismantled.

The village has a few shops including a post office, the Fox and Hounds and a primary school. The village retains a village green and there is a mix of housing. There is a large industrial estate south of the River Ogmore and a smaller one north of the river in the bend once occupied by the woollen mill and brewery.

West of the village are the Ynysawdre schools.

North of the village is Bryngarw House and gardens. The farmhouse came into the possession of Morgan Popkin Traherne in 1830 who transformed it into a Tudor style mansion. In 1775 John Popkin of Coytrahen House had given the house to his sister Frances on her marriage into the Traherne family. The gardens were laid out in the 1920s before the property was sold to R. S. Hayes, a Bridgend businessman in the 1940s. In 1961 the estate was purchased by the County Council and it was eventually decided to create a country park with the house converted into a country house hotel. There are woodland walks, formal and ornamental gardens with a lake and ponds attracting some 50,000 visitors a year.

Burry Green

Burry Green is a small hamlet a mile and a half north-west of Reynoldston in the Gower. There is a mix of older and modern housing and the village green with a pond.

Opposite the green is Bethesda Calvinistic Methodist Chapel, which was the centre for Calvinism in Gower. The chapel and adjoining manse were funded by Diana, Lady Barham who had moved from Kent to reside at Fairy Hill mansion to the east of Burry Green. Opened in 1814, the chapel was initially staffed by ministers of the Countess of Huntingdon's Connexion before a permanent minister was appointed. In 1821 Lady Barham broke with the Calvinists to join the Independents, but following her death in 1823, Lord Barham supported the appointment, in 1824, of William Griffiths who remained at Burry Green until his death in 1861. Known as the Apostle of Gower, Griffiths a native of Clydau in Pembrokeshire had been sent by the Association of Methodists as a missionary to the English speaking residents of Gower. In total, Lady Barham financed six chapels in Gower.

Fairy Hill is today a country house hotel. It was previously known as Peartree and came into the ownership of Richard Lucas in 1720. John Lucas renamed the property Fairy Hill in 1795 and it was leased by Lady Barham in 1813. Following her death in 1823 Henry Lucas occupied the property and it passed through several families until 1982 when it was purchased by the Frayne family and after considerable restoration was opened as a hotel in 1984.

To the north of Fairy Hill was Stackpool Mill, a corn mill operational from before 1665 until 1915. The only mill on the Burry stream, the structure was rebuilt in 1965.

Cadoxton Juxta Neath *Welsh Llangatwg*

Cadoxton Juxta Neath is so-called to differentiate it from Cadoxton Juxta Barry in the Vale of Glamorgan. It was once a very large parish stretching from the Breconshire border at Pontneddfechan to the sea. There were formerly a number of large houses in the village including Cadoxton Lodge the summer residence of George Tennant, the owner of the Tennant Canal and developer of the Port Tennant area of

Swansea. Tennant's granddaughter, the artist Dorothy Tennant married Henry Morton Stanley and they resided in the village at one time.

Today there is a mix of housing with modern estates.

The church of St Catwg was rebuilt in 1839-42. It is a large church, double aisled with chancel and a western tower. In the graveyard alongside a path is a 'murder' stone with the inscription 'Although the SAVAGE MURDERER escape for a season the detection of man, yet GOD hath set his mark on him either for time or eternity, and the cry of blood will assuredly pursue him to certain and terrible but righteous JUDGEMENT' under the heading of 'Murder'. The grave commemorates Margaret Williams, a native of Carmarthenshire who was in service in the parish. She was murdered in 1822 at the age of 26 and although a man was arrested he was not prosecuted because of lack of evidence and subsequently left for America. Apparently Margaret was pregnant and had gone for a walk with her lover, the cowman at Gelliau Farm where she worked.

Cliffe commented "Cadoxton Church is remarkable for a monument containing the pedigree of the family of Williams, engraved on sheets of copper, a copy of which occupies four large pages of Evans's Tour. The proverb 'as long as a Welsh pedigree' is here palpably exemplified."

A tramway connected Gelliau Colliery to the Tennant Canal. The colliery was situated above Cadoxton and is now in the Craig Gwladys Country Park where the tramroad forms a footpath. Another tramway led to Rhydding Colliery which was in the area of Alexander Road.

Cadoxton was home to the Vale of Neath Brewery established in 1830. Situated in what is now Maes yr Hafod, it was taken over by Evan Evans of Briton Ferry in 1850 and renamed Evan Evans Bevan Ltd. It was brewing 1,000 barrels a week in 1860 but was taken over by Whitbread Breweries in 1967 and closed in 1970.

There are two pubs, the Orb and Sceptre and the Green Dragon, a tuck shop and primary school. Llangatwg Comprehensive School is between Cadoxton and Aberdulais.

A curious incident is recorded in the court records. In 1727 Evan John, of Cilybebyll, mason, having been at Neath market, went for the night to an inn called Ty'nyrheol, at Cadoxton Juxta Neath. At dead of night he was taken out of bed into another room, where were a number of men and women. There they pretended to try him for his life, as a thief, and so condemned him to be executed. They actually hanged him for a short space of time, but then let him down and made him sign a paper purporting 'to release them for such their outrageous doings'. Sworn at Cardiff, 15 April, 1727, before Richard Carter.

Caerau *Fortresses*

Caerau is situated some two miles north of Maesteg at the head of the Llynfi Valley. Industry started early in the area with the establishment of a spelter (zinc) works at what became Spelter in 1830. It was served by the Dyffryn Colliery and a horse drawn railway, the Dyffryn Llynfi Porthcawl Railway was built in 1828 and extended to Coegnant in 1830. It ran some 15 miles to Porthcawl. The spelter works closed in 1847, but the Dyffryn Colliery was in operation until the 1880s. In 1889 North's Navigation Collieries opened the Caerau Colliery and the village of Caerau followed. The Caerau Colliery produced steam coal at two pits and house coal at a third, employing up to 2,380 men. The colliery closed in 1979, the men being transferred to Coegnant Colliery at Nantyffyllon and St John's Colliery Maesteg.

Today there is a small industrial estate on the site of the old spelter works, but most employment is away from the village, either in Maesteg and Nantyffyllon or further afield in Bridgend.

With the influx of miners and their families came the places of worship and the pubs. Noddfa Welsh Baptist Chapel was built on Blaencaerau Road in 1898. It is no longer in use. Seion Welsh Independent Chapel was built on Caerau Road in 1897 but is no longer in use. Bethel Welsh Wesleyan Methodist Chapel was built on Wesley Street in 1857and rebuilt in 1906 but is no longer in use. Hermon Calvinistic Methodist Chapel was built on Dyffryn Road in 1851 and rebuilt in 1897. It too has closed and despite standing next to the police station has been vandalized. Hope Baptist Chapel was built on Dyffryn Road in 1901 in the Arts and Crafts style. It has been demolished. Bethany Calvinistic Methodist Chapel on Hermon Road was built in 1852 and enlarged in 1903. It is no longer in use. Dyffryn

Welsh Independent Chapel was built on Bedw Street in 1872, rebuilt in 1898 and refurbished in 1905. The date stone reads 1897 and the chapel is still in use. St Cynfelin's Church was built in 1908-10 by the Cardiff Architect George Eley Halliday. The church in a Romanesque style has a twin aisled nave with chancel and vestry and an offset western bellcote. It was named after St Cynfelyn ab Bleiddud ab Meirion ab Tybiawn ab Cunedda Wledig. He was brother to St Cynydyn, and a distant relative of St David. He became a hermit living in Ceredigion. The hall next to the church was originally built as a mission church and is shown on the 1899 map.

The Blaencaerau Hotel was built in the 19th century at the top of the valley. It was renovated and renamed the Monkey Inn in the 1980s but was destroyed by fire after it had closed in 1990. The Blaenllynfi Hotel, Navigation Inn, Llynfi Coach House and Station Hotel remain together with a number of clubs.

Both cinemas, the Cosy on Library Road and the Coliseum, which was near the War Memorial, have disappeared. Caerau has a range of small shops and a supermarket, an infants and primary school.

Few signs of the coal industry remain and there has been a reclamation of the old waste sites. The village has its football and rugby pitches and open land around. There has been relatively little modern development apart from the Tudor and Blaencaerau estates.

Caswell

Caswell is a small hamlet overlooking the beautiful Caswell Bay at the south-eastern end of the Gower. East of the beach is a large chalet park while houses line the road that climbs to the west. Above the bay once stood Victoria Villa, later the Caswell Bay Hotel, demolished in the 1990s to make way for three apartment blocks. At the western side of the bay is Redley Cliff with an apartment block and on the headland are the outlines of Caswell Cliff Iron Age hillfort. At the foot of Redley Cliff is a large 19th century concrete water tank which was used in conjunction with a wind pump above the cliff to collect water from a spring and supply it to the houses above. Described on an Admiralty chart as a 'Notation Pumping Station', the windmill was demolished in the 1930s after a fire.

Cefn Cribwr *Ridgeback*

Cefn Cribwr as the name suggests is a village strung out along a ridge running between Aberkenfig and Kenfig Hill. There are views across the Bristol Channel to North Somerset beyond. Originally a ribbon development, there are a number of small housing estates built north and south of the B4281 road.

The area to the north of the village was mined by the monks of Margam Abbey and is still the site of extensive opencast mining. In the late 1770s a Birmingham industrialist, John Bedford opened an ironworks with a charcoal fuelled blast furnace. It remained in operation until 1836 and the remains include a blast furnace, charring ramp, three calcining kilns, a casting house and blowing engine house, built to take a Boulton and Watt type steam engine. The area is now a scheduled monument and Bedford Park offers the visitor an opportunity to explore the ruins.

Bedford also opened a number of coal mines, including the Cefn Slip Colliery opened to the east of Bedford Park in the 1860s. It was worked until 1918, employing up to 470 men, but was eventually closed due to flooding.

The small Cefn Cribwr Wesleyan Methodist Chapel was built in 1886. Siloam Welsh Independent Chapel was built off Bedford Road in 1829 and rebuilt in 1854. Nebo Welsh Baptist Chapel was built in 1848 and rebuilt in 1868, while Calvary English Baptist Chapel was built in 1905.

St Colman Bishop of Lindisfarne's church was built in 1925, but it was not consecrated until a refurbishment in 2005, after which it was permitted to conduct marriage services for the first time. The church is a red brick building with the appearance of a village hall rather than a church.

The Bethlehem Church Life Centre opened in 2005, and in addition to a church offers a conference venue, computer training facilities, a gymnasium and function centre. The church is described as 'non-religious, naturally supernatural and incredibly fun to be in.'

Cefn Cribwr Welfare Hall opened in 1924, funded by the Miners' Welfare Fund. Today it is a Council owned community centre.

The village has a post office, primary school and the Farmers Arms, Three Horseshoes and the White Lion in Bedford Road.

Cheriton

Cheriton is a small farming village in north-west Gower. Its church of St Cadog, known as the cathedral of Gower, is a 13th century building, restored in 1846 and 1874. The nave, tower, and chancel are 13th century with 19th century vestry and south porch. Of particular interest are the wall and ceiling paintings. It is thought that the church replaced one at nearby Landimore which had been affected by the encroachment of the sea.

North Hills Farm is a quail farm.

Glebe Farmhouse next to the church is an important medieval house with its original hall roof. It has an outshut-staircase, i.e. the staircase wall extends beyond the normal wall line, and a solar chimney designed to improve ventilation.

Burry Pill which flows through the village was used to drive three corn mills and a woollen mill and one of the leats constructed can still be seen. A forge existed near the village hall and Britannia Inn at the western end of the village.

Trinity Calvinistic Methodist Chapel was built as a school in 1817 but was in use as a chapel by 1824 when William Griffiths became the minister. The little chapel was rebuilt in 1868.

To the north of the village is an Iron Age promontory fort, known as North Hill Tor or Nottle Hill Tor Camp. A 250 foot embankment protects the fort from the south though the northern escarpment overlooking the estuary has been eroded by quarrying.

Cilfrew

Cilfrew is a village two miles north of Neath on a by-road to the Dulais valley. The spelling is an Anglicised form of Cil-ffriw meaning hilltop retreat. There has been considerable development in recent years on land to the west of the main road, taking advantage of the views offered over the Neath valley.

There was small scale mining carried on above the village which ceased in 1931. There was also a tin works, all evidence of which has disappeared.

Hermon Calvinistic Methodist Chapel was built in 1881 and Pisgah Independent Chapel is dated 1930.

Cilfrew was home to the Penscynor Wildlife Park which was open from 1971 to 1998. Built in the gardens of Penscynor House for the personal pleasure of the owner Idris Hale, the park attracted 200,000 visitors a year to see its collection of animals and birds. The site has been developed for housing and the house as a residential home.

Cilmaengwyn *White Stone Retreat*

Cilmaengwyn is a small village originally stretching along the Swansea Valley road between Pontardawe and Ystalyfera. It is now bypassed by the A4067 and in the 1950s a well spaced housing estate was built to the north of the main road. There is a post office but no other amenity. The 1877 map shows just two farms, Cilmaengwyn Isaf and Cilmaengwyn Uchaf to the north of the present village.

Cilybebyll *The Retreat of the Tents*

Cilybebyll is a tiny village perched above the Tawe Valley a mile and a half north-east of Pontardawe. The parish once covered a large area, but the village has just a few houses and the church of St John the Evangelist. Constructed on a Celtic *llan*, the church is medieval in origin but was subject to major Victorian restoration. There is the base of a Celtic preaching cross and the 1914 east window is by Clayton and Bell in memory of Herbert Lloyd of Plâs Cilybebyll. There is a squat tower, nave, chancel, south porch and a north transept.

Rees gives a history of the "old mansion of KILYBEBILL, the seat of John Herbert Lloyd, Esq. It was for a long period the property of a branch of the Herbert family, the last of whom, an heiress, conveyed it by marriage to Jenkin Turberville, Esq. of Ewenny, who made it his principal residence. At her death Mrs. Turberville bequeathed the estate by will to the present worthy owner. The house, which had fallen considerably into decay, has undergone a thorough repair, and now forms a very comfortable habitation." Plâs Cilybebyll is now a guest house.

In 2011 Cilybebyll hit the news when the small Gleision Colliery situated a mile and a half north-east of the village flooded with the loss of four lives.

Clydach

Clydach today is a large village with a population in excess of 12,000, six miles north of Swansea. It takes its name from the river, one of a number named Clydach, thought to have the same derivation as the River Clyde in Scotland, meaning a river flowing through a place of shelter.

By 1879 Clydach was a village of some size with a woollen factory, tin plate works, foundry, a tramway from Craig Cefn Parc collieries, the Swansea Vale Railway and the Swansea Canal. The opening of Ludwig Mond's Mond Nickel Company's refinery in 1902 saw a major boost to the economy and population of the village. The works remains the largest nickel refinery in Europe. A statue of Sir Ludwig Mond, who although German by birth was a British National who had established chemical works in north-west England, by Edouard Lanteri is to be found opposite the entrance to the works on Pontardawe Road.

Clydach has a good range of shops and supermarkets in the High Street. There are infants and primary schools as well as a range of pubs and clubs.

The non conformist chapels thrived in the village in the 19th and early 20th centuries, but the fall in the number of Welsh speakers in particular, has led to chapels and churches becoming redundant. Carmel Welsh Independent Chapel on Heol y Nant was built in 1901 but is now closed. Salem Fardre Calvinistic Methodist Chapel on Lone Road was built in 1871 and modified 1891. It is now closed. Bethel Evangelical Clydach Wesleyan Methodist Church was situated on the corner of Quarry Drive and Clydach Road. It is now a private dwelling. The first Hebron Independent Chapel was built in 1821 on a site later occupied by the Cloth Hall. In 1849 a larger chapel was built on Hebron Road, only to be replaced in 1882 by the even larger building which now stands on Hebron Road. It has now been converted into a private dwelling. Bethania Particular Baptist Chapel was built in 1841 on Heol Graig Felen and is now only used for burials. Capel y Cwar was built in 1795 on Bethania Road as an Arminian church but the worshippers switched to Bethania, the two chapels uniting in 1854. The congregation became too large for Bethania and Calfaria Baptist Chapel was built on the High Street to accommodate the congregation and opened in 1869. Bryn Salem Baptist Chapel was built in 1777, and later became known as Salem. The chapel was rebuilt and enlarged in 1815 but is no longer in existence.

There were two Anglican churches in Clydach. The older, St John's was opened in 1847 and was Welsh speaking. Built by the Neath architect William Whittington, it has a large northern porch cum transept with bellcote, a nave, choir and chancel. In 1905 the church of St Mary the Virgin was consecrated. Described at the time as the daughter church, it was a much larger building designed by E. M. B. Vaughan of Cardiff. It has a prominent tower, a triple aisled nave, chancel, and north and south transepts. St John's church is no longer in use.

Additionally there is St Benedict's Roman Catholic Church, a Jehovah's Witnesses' Kingdom Hall and Calvary Full Gospel Church of the Assemblies of God.

Clyne

Clyne is a small village in the Neath valley south of Resolven on the eastern side of the river. The name is difficult, but possibly derived from 'clyn', a place covered in bracken. The Clyne Colliery was operating in 1881 but by 1899 the colliery site to the south of the present village was occupied by the Resolven Tinplate Works. The works closed in the 1930s, but spurred the initial development of the village which expanded with new housing in the 1950s and 60s, though building since has been minimal. The railway line runs to the east of the village while the river and the Neath Canal run to the west. The canal crosses the river here by way of an aqueduct.

The village had two chapels, Hermon Independent Chapel in Tonclwyda was built in 1882, but Coshen Calvinistic Methodist Chapel in Heol Nant has disappeared without trace.

To the east of the village is the site of the Old Colliery, in scrub to the south of Clyne Farmhouse.

On the hill to the south of the village are two sets of cairns. There are eight at Cefn Ffordd and three at Gwenffrwd, all of unknown date as they have been disturbed, but following the line of a track between two Roman Forts, one in Melincourt and the other in Tonna.

Coed Darcy *Darcy Woods*

Coed Darcy is a planned new village on the site of the Llandarcy oil refinery, the first in the United Kingdom to process crude oil. Built between 1918 and 1922 it continued in production until 1997.

It is anticipated that the village will eventually contain 4,000 homes, and four schools.

Coity

Coity is a village to the north of Bridgend, now almost subsumed by the spread of the town, yet as late as 1811, it was deemed more important than its neighbouring town which was described as the 'Lower Hamlet of Coyty Parish'. The name is thought to derive from 'Coed Tŷ' or house of the woods.

Coity is considered a Norman settlement, but there are earthworks near the castle suggestive of a Roman fort while to the north is Coedparcgarw burial chamber dating from the Neolithic period, with its capstone still partially supported.

Coity Castle was originally built of timber in the early 12th century by Payn de Turberville, nicknamed the 'Demon', on the site of an

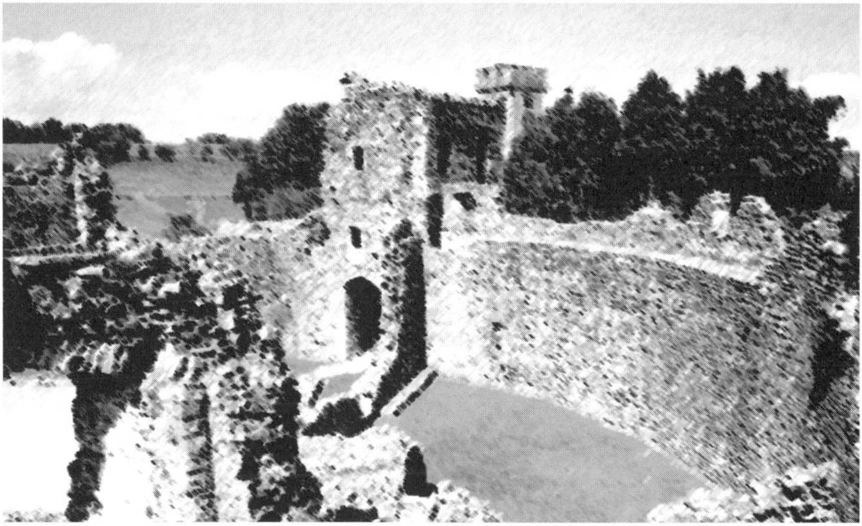

Coity Castle

earlier Welsh fortification. Thomas Rees comments “The ruins are among the most extensive and magnificent of any in South Wales, and are second in this respect lo Caerphili alone.” The Turberville name is listed in the Roll of Battle Abbey, though there were other members of the family settling in other parts of the country. Robert Fitzhamon took possession of Glamorgan after the defeat of Rhys ap Tewdor in 1093 and distributed the Glamorgan Lordships among his twelve knights. According to legend, Turberville alone was forced to acquire his own lands and challenged the Welsh Chieftain Morgan ap Meurig who offered him the choice of battle or the marriage of his daughter Sibylla to gain the lands. There is possibly some confusion as some hundred years later Gilbert de Turberville gained Landymor in Gower as the result of his marriage to Matilda, daughter of the Welsh lord of Afan, Morgan Gam and subsequently acquired the manor of Newcastle from Morgan Gam. Sir Payn de Turberville held the Lordship of Coity on the tenure of ‘serjeantry of hunting’, giving him the right to the Lordship without military service. Together with the Castles at Newcastle and Ogmore, Coity formed a formidable presence. It was replaced by a stone fortification in 1180 and further strengthened in the 14th century after Sir Lawrence Berkerolles inherited the Lordship of Coity in 1384. The castle was strong enough to resist Owain Glyndwr at the start of the 15th century. According to Thomas Wilkins in his *Tales and Sketches* (1879), Berkerolles was murdered by his wife, Matilda le Despenser in 1411. His widow confessed the crime and was sentenced to be buried alive. There are however discrepancies in the account. Matilda’s father, Sir Thomas le Despenser is described as an old man, whereas he was beheaded in 1400 at the age of 27, and there is no record of his having a daughter named Matilda. (Wilkins makes reference to Iolo Morganwg as his source and it has been shown that Morganwg invented much of his history.) In 1411 the castle passed to the Gamage family, but with the marriage of Barbara Gamage to Sir Robert Sydney, Earl of Leicester in 1584 the castle was abandoned and fell into ruin. Today it is in the care of Cadw and is open 10a.m to 4 p.m. year round with free admission.

The church of St Mary the Virgin dates from the 14th century and its importance can be gathered from the crossing tower. It is thought that the initial building was done by the builders of the castle and completed in 1325. There were additions in the 16th century and a refurbishment in 1860. Among the 14th century effigies is one of Sir Payn de Turberville. Rees reports "On opening a grave in the chancel of Coity church for the interment of the late rector, Dr. Richards, a vault was discovered containing the bodies of Sir Payne Turburville and his lady. From the inscription it appeared that the knight was to remain in purgatory forty days!"

One sad tale from the past is recorded in the court records, when in 1725 "Elizabeth Moses, of Coyty, aged two years, fell into a pan full of ale and was drowned."

Today the village has expanded considerably and has a primary school and pub, the Six Bells. The area around the castle and church retains some older buildings with Gilead Independent Chapel built in 1826 and refurbished in 1862.

Cornelly

Cornelly is divided between the villages of North Cornelly and South Cornelly, now split by the M4.

Always two separate villages, North Cornelly was originally known as The Vill of Walter Lupellus and was centred around a medieval stronghouse, Old Hall which now stands in trees to the east of the school. It appears that the name of North Cornelly emerged from its proximity to Cornelly which subsequently became known as South Cornelly. Some believe the name Cornelly to be derived from St Cornelius, though there is no evidence of a church in either village and a more likely derivation is from the Norman Thomas de Cornell who gave ten acres of arable land to Neath Abbey. The main industry was quarrying which is still carried on to the east of South Cornelly.

North Cornelly expanded rapidly in the 20th century and is today far the larger of the villages with a number of housing developments. It has a school and a range of shops and supermarkets. It has two pubs. The New House Inn which was shown as a public house on the 1899 map stands next to the Cornelly Arms, now a private house while opposite once stood the Old House pub. The modern Green Acres pub, restaurant and motel is situated on Heol Fach.

Old Hall was altered in the 18th century, but in the garden are bee boles, a wall with recesses for bees, giving greater shelter than a hive. Capel-y-Pil, Pyle Calvinistic Methodist Chapel on Ffordd Yr Eglwys was built in 1786, to be replaced by a new building on an adjacent site in 1830. This too was replaced in 1862 by a new chapel, built on the site of the original, the 1830 chapel becoming a schoolroom. The chapel was declared redundant and put up for sale in 2011 and has been acquired by the community. The modern North Cornelly Methodist Church stands on Heol Fach. There is also a modern place of worship on Greenfield Terrace squeezed in between two bungalows.

South Cornelly has also seen expansion in the latter part of the 20th century, but on a much smaller scale than its neighbour. The village has been by-passed and has a small industrial estate to the south where there is a service station, Indian restaurant and garden centre. The old horse drawn railway from Maesteg to Porthcawl (later the Great Western Railway) used to pass through the village and the pub, the Three Horseshoes was originally known as the Horse and Tram. The pub has now been converted to a recording studio.

Coychurch

Coychurch today is a large village between the Bridgend Industrial Estate and the M4 motorway. The name is thought to be a corruption of Coed Church meaning a woodland church. There have been substantial building developments over the last 50 years. The heart of the village however remains attractive with its pubs and the large church of St Crallo, from which the Welsh name Llangrallo derives.

The present church of St Crallo dates from the 13th century, but the site was in use prior to the Norman Conquest. According to Sabine Baring-Gould, St Crallo was born around 535AD the son of St Sadwrn and St Canna, the patron of the neighbouring parish of Llangan. A pupil of his uncle, St Illtyd at Llantwit Major, the church at Coychurch is the only one dedicated to him. According to Iolo Morganwg St Canna was buried at Coychurch, the parish in which Iolo's own mother was born. A Celtic cross in the churchyard was according to Samuel Lewis almost identical to the circular cross at Llantwit Major with the name of St Samson and the carver Samuel decipherable. Only the shaft now remains, the circular cross apparently having been damaged when the tower collapsed. There is also the 9th century Stone of Ebissar.

The Grade I Listed church is large, often referred to as the mini cathedral of the Vale. It is Cruciform with a three aisled nave, and a crossing tower, a feature normally associated with important churches and cathedrals. Lewis reported that the church was in a poor state of repair in 1833 and indeed the tower collapsed in 1876 after a contractor disturbed the foundations when moving some 1,800 skulls to another part of the graveyard, requiring the rebuilding of the tower, south transept and part of the choir. The nave was also rebuilt in the 19th century. The windows in the nave are from 1963 by Frank Roper. Various wall paintings were destroyed when the tower collapsed and only the headless depiction of a saint remains in the south transept.

There was once a holy well, Ffynnon Grallo near the south side of the church.

The medieval Old Rectory in the grounds is now used as the Llandaff Diocesan Board of Finance Office. To the south of the church was the site of a 7th century theological college. The Rev. Thomas Richards, author of the first comprehensive Welsh-English dictionary, published in 1753, is buried in the graveyard.

The village has retained its two pubs, The White Horse and The Prince of Wales.

However, Hebron Welsh independent Chapel has disappeared.

North-east of the village is the Coed y Mwstwr Country House Hotel and Golf Club. The house was built in 1888. Within the village is a primary school, garage and hairdresser.

In 1692, according to court records, one, Edward Reece of Coychurch, a yeoman, with others seized and abducted Mary Taynton, a 10 year old girl in Cardiff. She was forcibly married to Reece in a house in Neath to gain ownership of her lands and tenements.

Coytrahen

Coytrahen is a village situated between Tondu and Maesteg. The name is shown on old maps as Goetre Hên, possibly meaning 'old dwelling in the woods'.

The Coytrahen estate was originally in two parts, each held by a different Powell family. It was united through the marriage of Hannah Powell to Anthony Powell. Their son, also Anthony inherited both estates and these passed to his nephew Morgan Popkin whose family owned land in Llansamlet. The Llansamlet land was sold to pay debts and the Popkins made their home at Coytrahen from 1736. The estates passed to Morgan Popkin Traherne around 1800. The Traherne family were living at Coytrahen House in 1848. Coytrahen House was built by John Popkin (died 1797) as a three storey mansion with single storey service wings which have been demolished, as has the upper floor of the main house. It was occupied for a time in the mid 19th century by Alexander Brogden (see Tondu) before being sold in 1948. Coytrahen Park Colliery situated in woods south-east of the house opened in 1906 with a second section opening in 1910. The coal was used for gas production and mining continued until 1928, with up to 389 men employed.

The village today has expanded from the terraces along the main road with a small estate to the west. The village retains its pub, the Nicholls Arms.

The church of St Thomas is relatively modern, with a single cell with western bellcote and south porch; it has now been converted to residential use as has the 1901 Wesleyan Methodist Chapel.

A mile and a quarter north-west of the village are the paper mills now operated by the Georgia Pacific company.

South of the mills lies Cefn Ydfa farm. This was the scene of one of the great romantic tragedies. Ann Thomas, the niece of Rhys Price of Tynton Llangeinor (father of Richard Price philosopher), was born in 1704 and fell in love with the local poet and thatcher Will Hopcyn. Ann however was a ward of Anthony Maddocks, a lawyer, following her father's death in 1706. It was decided that Ann was to be married to Maddocks' son, also Anthony. Ann was forbidden to see Hopcyn, but until it was discovered, they continued their love affair by letter. Hopcyn left the area and Ann and Anthony were married on 4th May, 1725. Ann however pined for Hopcyn and fell dangerously ill. She pleaded to see Hopcyn and at last her mother relented. Will returned in time for Ann to die in his arms in 1727. Their story was told in a 1904 film by William Haggar. Hopcyn died unmarried in 1741 and is credited with the words of the Welsh song *Bugeilio'r Gwenith Gwyn*

(Tending the White Wheat) used by Joseph Parry in one of his operas. Anthony Maddocks inherited the Thomas estate and remarried shortly after Ann's death. Ann and Will are buried at Llangynwyd.

Craig Cefn Parc *Park Behind the Rocks*

Craig Cefn Parc today is an attractive village above the wooded Cwm Clydach RSPB Nature Reserve and sheltered from the west by Mynydd Y Gwair.

A former mining village, there are the remains of tramways that connected to the Cwm Clydach Railway.

There were a number of mines in the area including the Clydach Merthyr Colliery, opened as the Western Merthyr Slant Colliery in 1863. It continued in production until 1961, employing up to 593 men. Gas free and with a sandstone roof, it had an underground blacksmith shop and boilers. It remained open until 1978 however, as a means of ventilating and pumping the Graig Merthyr Colliery some three miles to the west in the Dulais Valley. The Graigola Colliery was started in 1850 and closed in 1929.

Elim Baptist Chapel was built in 1891 and Pantycrwys Independent Congregationalist built as a school in 1862, rebuilt in 1869 and 1880 and modified in 1896.

There has been considerable modern building in recent years and the village has a post office, school and, on Clydach Road, the New Inn.

Croeserw

Croeserw is situated in the upper Afan Valley off the mountain road between Cymer and Caerau in the Llynfi Valley. It takes its name from Croeserw Farm, 'croeserw' meaning 'cross acres'. Until 1945 this was a small village on the A4107, but following the Second World War there was a large amount of building of social housing on the hillside above the original village. Many of the houses are now privately owned, but the village suffers from the impression of drab uniformity typical of early post war developments. Croeserw also has a high crime rate (550 crimes recorded in 2012 in a population of 1600), and was described as the 'The Sickest Place in Britain' by the *Western Mail*.

There is a post office, shop, pub, community centre, primary school and light industrial estate.

East of the village once stood the Glenavon Colliery, opened in 1899. It never employed more than 180 men and was not worked by the National Coal Board.

On the edge of woodland to the west of the village are the remnants of a Bronze Age cairn, some sixty feet in diameter but now just two feet high.

The mountains around the village are set to become major wind farms.

Crofty

Crofty situated on the north coast of Gower is a village that has seen considerable expansion since 1960. The derivation of the name is uncertain, but is thought to originate in the Welsh 'y groft wrth y tŷ?' meaning the small field near the house. The oldest and most attractive part of the village is around Chapel Road and Forge Road. The Crofty Inn, said to be the oldest house in the village and a former farmhouse, is found in Forge Road. Zoar Presbyterian Church was built in 1884 and rebuilt in 1906. There was a corn mill at the end of Chapel Road where the modern 'Mill House' now stands. During the 19th century there was coal mining in the village with the Dulas and Penlan collieries situated to the north-east of the village near the rugby ground and industrial estate but apart from some terraced cottages all evidence of this has disappeared.

There is an extensive industrial estate, part of which is devoted to the production of Penclawdd Cockles, a sought after delicacy in the Swansea area. Stretching into the marshes to the north of the industrial estate is Salthouse Point, at the end of which was thought to be the salthouse, for the storing of salt which would have been extracted from the seawater.

Crynant

Crynant is a village in the Dulais valley, some eight miles north-east of Neath. The anglicized name of the village is from Creunant, the stream that flows through the village to the Dulais.

A chapel of ease was established here by the monks of Neath Abbey who also had a monastic grange here. Parts of the chapel date back to the 13th century. It was rebuilt at the turn of the 19th century and is now used as a chapel of rest. The new church of St Margaret was built by the Neath architect J. Cook-Rees and has a double aisled nave, chancel, vestry, organ loft, a west door, south porch and a double sanctus bellcote. It was originally built as a chapel of ease but subsequently became a parish church. The stained glass windows are from the 1950s and 60s and designed by Celtic Studios.

The village changed dramatically in the 19th and early 20th centuries with the expansion of the coal industry. The first colliery was Maes Mawr, to the east of the village opened in 1874. The Cefn Coed and Blaenant collieries followed in the 20th century. Cefn Coed was the world's deepest anthracite mine. It was also one of the most dangerous, earning it the name of 'The Slaughterhouse'. The collieries at their height employed over 1000 men but the last pit closed in 1990. Today the Cefn Coed Colliery Museum provides an insight into the industry. The above ground workings are intact and there is a simulated gallery but no access to the underground workings which include ten miles of underground roadway. The museum stands on the A4109 half a mile south of the village and is open daily in the summer with free admission.

With the increase in population came the non-conformist chapels, attendance at which increased with the 1905 religious revival. Bethania Baptist Chapel was built in 1907 in Woodland Road but has now been demolished. Saron Independent chapel was built in 1904, Capel Bethel Welsh Wesleyan Methodist Chapel in School Road was built in 1921 and rebuilt in 1933. Salem Methodist Chapel in Brynawel was built in 1773, rebuilt in 1867 and again in 1937 in the Arts and Crafts style. Zion Calvinistic Methodist chapel in Neath Road was built in 1821 and rebuilt in 1868 by the architect W. Herbert. It is no longer in use as a chapel. North of the village, Godre'r Rhos Independent Chapel was built in 1753 and rebuilt in 1855 by the architect Thomas Thomas of Landore.

A temporary resident of Crynant in the 1840s was Alfred Russell Wallace, the evolutionist. He described his time in the village: "The parish being so extensive we had to stay at many different points for convenience of the survey, and one of these was about five miles up the Dulais valley, where we stayed at a small beershop in the hamlet of Crynant I was often here alone for weeks together, and saw a good deal of the labourers and farmers, few of whom could speak any English. The landlady here brewed her own beer in very primitive fashion in a large iron pot or cauldron in the washhouse, and had it ready for sale in a few days – a rather thick and sweetish liquor, but very palatable. The malt and hops were bought in small quantities as wanted, and brewing took place weekly, or even oftener, when there was a brisk demand."

The village once had a railway station, but while the line is still in use it is for goods trains only. Crynant is a long village but with plenty of greenery is less densely populated than many former mining villages. It has shops, including Segadelli's sweet shop, a school, community centre, post office and the Gradon public house in what used to be the British Legion. The Kingfisher Inn to the north of the village was for sale as a 'Former Public House' while the Red Lion, the oldest hostelry in the village closed in 2007.

North-east of the village are a number of cairns thought to be Bronze Age, near Gelli Benuchel, the site of the medieval Creunant Grange. To the south of the village was the manor corn mill while to the east runs Sarn Helen, the Roman road from Neath to Brecon.

Cwmafan/Cwmavon *Afan Valley*

Cwmafan is a large village north of Port Talbot incorporating the areas of Brynbryddan and Ynysygwas.

North of the village is the Bronze Age Foel Fynyddau cairn, while to the east are the Pen y Castell and Mynydd Emroch enclosures, thought to be Iron Age.

To the west of the village on Mynydd Dinas are the remains of Castell Bolan, a motte and bailey castle of which the motte consists of a 10 foot banked mound with a further 10 foot mound on it, some 90 foot in diameter.

The site of Ynys Afan, a grange of Margam Abbey, is believed to have been located at the base of Ynysygwas Hill.

The village became a centre for industry in the 19th and early 20th centuries with an increase in population. There were gas works, brickworks, chemical works, coal mines, copper and iron works. Most signs of the industries of the village have disappeared under modern developments and even streets like Pelly Street and Gower Street have disappeared. Copper was produced from 1838 to 1906 and to combat the pollution, a flue was built to take the gasses to a chimney built on Foel Fynyddau a mile to the north. Metal particles in the fumes were deposited in the flue and then collected and re-used. The pollution moved to the hillside which became poisoned resulting in the deaths of sheep and cattle. The chimney stack was destroyed in 1940 as it was regarded as a landmark for German pilots bombing Swansea, while the flue was damaged during cable laying.

St Michael's Church has a tower dating back to 1660, though the church is much older in origin, dating from the 12th century. There was a restoration in the 19th century by the Llandaff architect John Prichard. The altar is particularly interesting, being composed of an Elizabethan chamber tomb with engravings of the children of the deceased and topped by a marble altar table. The church has a double aisled nave with chancel and south porch. The tower has a yellow brick spire which was added in the 18th century.

Services at St Michael's were conducted in Welsh and to accommodate the influx of English speakers, a new English church was built as a chapel of ease to St Michael's in 1856. All Saints was designed by John Prichard and built on the site of the former grange of Ynys Afan. The church had a spire and the bell was cast at the Cwmavon Works at a cost of 60 guineas. It was refurbished in 1978 but demolished in 2009 and the site is now commemorated by All Saints Place.

Another place of worship which has given way to modern housing was Pelly Street Primitive Methodist chapel, built in 1848. Seion Independent Chapel was built in 1821 and rebuilt in 1850. On Cwmavon Road near its junction with London Row, it too has been demolished.

Rock Independent Chapel was founded in 1840 and rebuilt in 1870 in the Arts and Crafts style. Penuel Baptist chapel was first built in 1844 and rebuilt in 1856 and again in 1908. It is in a neo-gothic style with the front flanked by two staircase towers topped by small spires.

Rock Baptist Chapel was built in 1838 but has now been demolished. Bethania Baptist Chapel was originally built in 1850 and then rebuilt in 1858. Tabernacle Calvinistic Methodist Chapel was built in 1854 and rebuilt in 1873.

The village today is a suburb of Port Talbot. There are a number of pubs, shops and a post office, a library and primary school. There has been a great deal of building in recent years and the village has a wide range of housing built over the last 180 years. Gradually the surrounding valley is returning to its former wooded beauty.

Cwmfelin *Mill Valley*

The 1877 map of the area places Cwmfelin, a village to the south of Maesteg, to the east of the present village. It was originally situated between the railway and the River Llynfi, which was crossed by Pont y Tinker. The village now runs along the Bridgend to Maesteg road. There is a village primary school and a convenience store. There has been a major development of modern housing between the main road and the valley. Libanus Methodist Chapel was built in 1861 and rebuilt in 1871 but has since been demolished. Calfaria Welsh Baptist Chapel on Mill Street was built in 1877 and is still in use. Noddfa Welsh Independent Chapel in Mill Street has been demolished and a house built on the site. Ebenezer Independent Chapel, Bridgend Road, was built in 1868, modified in 1911, and derelict by 1998.

Cwmgors *Marsh Valley*

Cwmgors is a largely ribbon development along the A474 Ammanford to Pontardawe road. A former mining village, the Cwmgors Colliery was started in 1880 near Gorse Lane by a local shopkeeper, Joseph Thomas. Initially a small operation employing just 16 men in 1896, it was serviced by horse and cart until a new rail line opened in 1901. It was taken over and expanded, employing 410 miners at its peak. It closed in 1964 and all trace has disappeared.

St Mary's church was opened in 1886. It has a nave, chancel, south porch and western bellcote.

Seion Baptist chapel was started in 1894. Situated opposite Parc Howard Road, Tabernacle Independent Chapel was built between 1888 and 1912. An impressive building in the Gothic style, it has a triple entry through the gable end. Much of the ornate brick and stonework to the sides is obscured by trees and bushes and the close proximity to housing. There was a chapel, known as Hen Gapel to the west of the present village, across the county border in Carmarthenshire. Built first as a schoolroom in 1762, then as Carmel chapel in 1822, it remained active despite New Carmel being built in Gwaun Cae Gurwen in 1877. It was renovated in 1927, but was destroyed by fire and no trace is now visible.

The present village has a good mix of housing, a primary school, mini supermarket and takeaway and TJ's Tavern. There is a small industrial estate

Cwmllynfell *Valley of the Silent Water*

Cwmllynfell is a former mining village on the southern slopes of the Black Mountain between Brynaman and Ystalyfera. The village is currently in Neath Port Talbot County, but in the past part has been in Breconshire.

Reynolds and Aubrey opened a drift mine here in 1820 which continued until 1880. In 1825 an explosion killed 59 miners. In 1908 the colliery was reopened and continued in operation until 1959 employing up to 396 men. To the west of the village there is an opencast mining operation.

The Swansea Vale Railway between Swansea and Brynamman Station skirted the village to the east, but passenger services ceased in 1960 and freight shortly thereafter.

The village has a good mix of housing with plenty of open space including a park, tennis courts and rugby ground. There is the community hall, social club, primary school, mini supermarket and post office. There is also the Black Mountain Gallery offering artwork by Welsh contemporary artists Mark Lloyd Williams and Muriel Williams.

Rehoboth Apostolic Chapel was built in 1953 at the western end of the village. A Baptist Chapel once stood where the car park at the entrance to Is Y Bryniau is today. The Methodist Chapel in Cae Du Road is now a private dwelling. Seion Cwmllynfell Independent Chapel was built in 1786 and rebuilt in 1814, 1823, 1860 and 1903.

Cymmer/Cymer *Meeting of rivers*

Cymer lies at the confluence of the Corrwg and Afan rivers and is at a cross roads with roads leading to Port Talbot, Glyncorrwg, Maesteg and the Rhondda Valley.

In 1877 there were a few terraces of houses, three inns, the Rock and Fountain, the Farmers Arms and the New Inn and Hebron Chapel. The main activities were quarrying and farming.

By 1900 the village had expanded with the coming of railways from Maesteg and the mining activities at Blaengwynfi. There was a railway station and post office and St John's Church. The Duffryn Rhondda Colliery opened in 1880 to the west of the village and at its peak employed over 1,300 men. It closed in 1967. The Glyncymmer Colliery opened in 1895 and gradually expanded. It employed up to 160 men before closing in 1932. The village saw further expansion in the early decades of the 20th century. After a period of decline the village is attracting new housing, taking advantage of its beautiful setting especially with the re-forestation of the valley.

The original Hebron Independent Chapel was one of the oldest buildings in the village and was built in 1794. After several modifications and rebuilds it was rebuilt in 1903; it is no longer in use. Calfaria Baptist Chapel was built in 1903 but is no longer in use. St John's Church has now been converted into a private dwelling. The United Free Methodist Chapel was built before 1918 and is still in use. Another chapel is now the Bryn Siriol Senior Citizens Centre. Bethania Methodist Chapel was built in 1895 and rebuilt in 1921, it is privately owned and redundant. St Joseph's Roman Catholic Church is still in use as is Gilgal Apostolic Church.

The village has a primary and secondary school, a swimming pool and sports hall and, unusually, a police station. The old GWR railway station is now the Refreshment Room pub and there is a garage and local store.

Cynonville

Cynonville in the Afan valley was originally named Cynonafan, but the name was changed in 1910 as part of a plan to build a garden village to attract workers to the area mine. Just two streets of substantial semi detached houses were built before the First World War intervened. (Cynon means chief brook.)

The Cynon Colliery was sunk in 1908 by the Cynon Colliery Company who employed 417 men. After the First World War the workforce declined substantially and at the time of nationalization there were just 22 men employed. The National Coal Board closed the colliery which was then worked under licence until the 1960s.

Some 300 yards south-west of the village is the Afan Argoed Forestry Visitor Centre and South Wales Miners' Museum. The Museum, a registered charity, is open during the period Easter to end October and staffed by volunteers. Exhibits include a Blacksmith Shop, Lamp Room and an Engine House. Afan Argoed Country Park is now called the Afan Forest Park and consists of 48 square miles of forest, containing what are regarded as the best mountain biking trails in Britain. There are walking trails , campsites and an open air theatre.

Above the museum was Argoed Colliery, started in the 1890s and at its peak employing 250 men. After nationalization it was worked under licence until 1953.

Tabernacle Baptist Chapel was built during the early 20th century between the village and the museum. It is now a private house.

Duffryn Rhondda

Duffryn Rhondda is a former mining village in the Afan valley, just above Cynonville. Like Cynonville it was planned as a garden village and the semi detached houses are similar. In two sections, the village is larger than Cynonville and has a post office and mini supermarket, school and the Afan Lodge Hotel. The hotel occupies the site of the former Duffryn and Cynon Welfare Hall and Institute which is where Richard Burton began his acting career.

The Duffryn Rhondda Colliery was situated in the valley just north-east of the village. Started in the 1880s, at its peak it employed 1660 men. This had fallen to 840 in 1945 and the colliery closed in 1967. An aerial ropeway was used to transport waste from the mine to the spoil heaps which unusually remain in place, though they are gradually being reclaimed by nature. There was also a quarry to the east of the village with a tramroad.

The small Seion Calvinistic Methodist chapel was built in 1922 with a flat roof.

Dunvant

Dunvant is a village four and a half miles north-west of Swansea. It was a coal mining area with the Voilart, Killan, Bishwell, Bryn Mawr and Dunvant Collieries operating in the area. Bishwell and Bryn Mawr closed in the 1870s and the Voilart site had become a brickworks by 1899. Dunvant closed in 1914 and Killan in 1925.

The commumity was bisected by the Swansea section of the London and North Western Railway and Dunvant had its own station. The course of the railway, running along the valley still splits the village, but provides an attractive green heart. Dunvant started as a ribbon development but expanded considerably from the 1960s. It does however maintain a great deal of open space and woodland.

Ebenezer Welsh Independent Chapel was built in 1872 and rebuilt in 1882 and 1893. There was a Wesleyan Methodist on the south side of Dunvant Road, built in 1882, but no longer in existence.

There are a number of small shops, two primary schools and The Dunvant public house. The old Dunvant Inn on Killan Road has disappeared. The Found Out which replaced it is derelict.

Dyffryn Cellwen *White Grove Vale*

Dyffryn Cellwen is a former mining village between the smaller villages of Onllwyn and Banwen at the top of the Dulais valley. The village offers views over the Brecon Beacons and has a school, mini supermarket, post office and pharmacy and The Dyffryn public house.

There were no mines in the village, but the drift mines of Onllwyn and Banwen were situated to the south and east. All mining ceased in 1964, to be followed by opencast operations which have also ceased and the land restored. Local employment is provided in the Onllwyn coal distribution depot which receives coal from the Selar opencast site above Blaengwrach and is then transported by rail.

St David's is a mission church, built of corrugated iron. Calfaria Baptist chapel was demolished and Noddfa Wesleyan Methodist Chapel closed.

Efail-fâch *Little Smithy*

Efail-fâch is shown on old maps as Gefail-fach. It is a village between Pontrhydyfen and Neath at the junction of the road to Tonmawr. There was once a corn mill on the Afon Polenna and the Colliers Arms is shown on the 1877 map though there was no colliery in the village. Sardis Welsh Independent Chapel was built in 1856 and rebuilt in 1905 above the railway bridge. It has since been demolished. Bryn Seion Calvinistic Methodist Mission Room, on the road to Tonmawr, was built during the late nineteenth century, but had fallen into disuse by 1984. Siloh Baptist Chapel was built prior to 1899.

There is a mix of housing with some modern housing set in an attractive valley with woodland on either side.

Felindre *Mill Town*

Felindre today is a small village in a rural setting, three miles east of Pontardulais. Situated at the confluence of the Lliw and Nant Ddu streams, the Felindre Corn Mill still stands with its machinery intact, including the 12 foot diameter overshot water wheel. It is still fed by a leat. Nebo Independent Chapel was built in 1824, rebuilt in 1857 and again in 1896. The name of a former cottage, Pandy would appear to denote that there was also a fulling mill in the village at some time. The village has a primary school and the Shepherds Country Inn and Stores, combining the role of village pub and shop.

North-east of the village are the two Lliw reservoirs providing attractive walks. The reservoirs are fed by a pipeline from the River Tawe at Nantgaredig and the flow of water in the Tawe is regulated by the Llyn Brianne Reservoir high in the Cambrian Mountains. Together, these form a complex water management system that supplies much of Glamorgan with fresh water.

Garden Village

Garden Village was an early 20th century housing estate of mainly semi detached properties on the eastern outskirts of Gorseinon. Originally 200 houses, it was extended in the second half of the 20th century.

The first foundations were laid in 1913 when the scheme was backed by a group of local businessmen. The houses were of high quality and by 1916 twenty pairs of semi detached houses had been completed on the south side of St Paul's Terrace, eleven in Garngoch Terrace, eight in Garden Crescent and two on Myrtle Road. Building stopped until after 1921. It had been intended to build St Paul's Church on St Paul's Terrace but, by 1935, the map shows a cruciform church on Swansea Road with a hall behind. Only the chancel appears to have been brick built, the church having been more of a temporary mission church structure which was demolished between 2003 and 2005, with only the hall remaining.

The village has a post office general store and takeaway.

Garnswllt *(Garn – Cairn or Heap, Swllt – Shilling)*

Garnswllt is a hamlet north of Pontardulais on the eastern side of the River Loughor. The village enjoys views over the valley and north to Ammanford.

A former mining village, though coal mining was on a small scale after the closure of the Garnswllt mine in 1875. The Garn No. 2 and Catham mines operated until 1972 and 1965 respectively. A further mine to the south at Tan y Garn was worked until 1990.

Garnswllt has lost its school pub and post office, but retains Noddfa Baptist Chapel built in 1841.

Heol y Mynydd rises to Mynydd y Gwair, giving views across Carmarthenshire and on a clear day into Pembrokeshire and Breconshire. The remote Gerazim Independent Baptist chapel dates from 1811. There are a number of Bronze Age cairns and round barrows on the mountain and a curious cairnfield south-west of Gerazim Chapel with eight mounds but thought to have been agricultural in nature rather than burial mounds.

Gelli-nudd *Neath Grove*

Situated on the A474 between Pontardawe and Neath, Gelli-nudd is a village of modern houses. In 1861 the Cwm Nant Llwyd Colliery was sunk to the south of the village and continued in operation until 1911, employing 218 men at its peak it closed in 1911. A tramway ran north down to the railway on the banks of the Tawe, and is commemorated in Tramway Road. The Nant Gelli Nudd powered a woollen factory, where Hen Felen or Old Mill stands today. There was a mixed school as early as 1877, even though there were very few houses. By 1918 the school had closed and the village now had an isolation hospital and a mission room which became Bryn Seion Chapel, now a private dwelling. Even by 1964 there were only a few houses along New Road though the name had by this time changed from Gelli Nedd to Gelli-nudd. Expansion took place in the 1980s with new bungalows and houses. In 2013 plans were announced to close Gelli-nudd Hospital which was used for the elderly.

Glais *Stream*

Glais today is an attractive semi rural village situated five miles north-east of Swansea city centre. Built partly on a hillside there is a good mix of housing with some modern developments. There is a school, village store and post office and two hostelries, the Globe Inn and the Old Glais Inn.

In 1879 the Glais Pit was situated on what is now Graigola Road. It had closed by 1899. Other industrial activity in the area was quarrying, a smithy and timber mill. The railway ran through the village, with a goods station opposite the Globe Inn on a branch line towards Neath. The Glais station was on the Swansea Vale line, off Station Road. A cottage an on Ynys-y-mond Road was originally built as the Ynyspenllwch Works School in 1862. The school closed in 1882 when Glais National School opened and the building was converted into two cottages and now a single cottage.

St Paul's Church was built in 1881 as a chapel of ease to Llansamlet, which explains its lack of burials. A disused barn was used as the basis for the church which has a nave, apsed chancel, vestry and western bellcote.

Peniel Welsh Baptist Chapel was built on Station Road in 1891 and closed in 1999.

Seion Independent Chapel in Ynys-y-mond Road was built in 1840 and rebuilt in 1865.

Glais was home to the Glais Stadium and racecourse. Dating from the mid 19th century it was used for horse racing, greyhound racing and athletics. A grandstand and more formal track was constructed after Swansea Council refused to allow greyhound racing at St Helens. The stadium has disappeared under Tawe Vale golf course and the A4067 road.

Glyncorrwg *Corrwg Glen*

Glyncorrwg is a former mining village set in the beautiful scenery of the Nant Corrwg valley in the upper Afan valley. The village predates the mining industry with the church of St John the Baptist thought to have been founded in the pre-Norman period. Above the village on Pen y waun are three Bronze Age Cairns.

In 1811 it was noted that the coal was mined for the consumption of the then 243 inhabitants of the parish.

Mining had started in a major way by the 1860s when the South Wales Mineral Railway connected Glyncorrwg to Briton Ferry though a tramroad connecting Blaen Cregan to the Neath Canal at Aberdulais some seven miles away had been in use since 1840. This tramroad made use of an incline engine as the line ran over the hill from the Neath valley rather than through a tunnel while the rest of the journey was achieved with twenty horses. There was a tramway from a quarry below Mynydd Resolven which met the railway where Heol y Deryn now stands. Near here was the site of the Welsh Main Colliery which was operational prior to 1875 when the area around Commercial Street had a hotel as well as Jenkins Arms, Nebo Independent Chapel and Bethel Baptist Chapel. The Lamb Inn was where Queen Street now stands, while there was a school above the church.

Mining expanded rapidly in the years surrounding 1900, with Blaencorrwg, Glyncorrwg, North Rhondda and Nantewlaeth Collieries operating in this small valley. The village expanded rapidly with up to 995 men employed in the Glyncorrwg Colliery alone in 1938.

With the increase in population came an increase in the chapels with Carmel Calvinistic Methodist Chapel 1875, United Free Methodist Chapel 1913, Bible Christian Chapel 1888 and Nebo Independent Chapel established in 1861. St John's Church was rebuilt in 1905 with a 15th century east window, a holy water stoup and the old font included in the new church which has a large double bellcote.

Glyncorrwg Workmen's Institute and Memorial Hall was opened in 1926 by Finlay A. Gibson, secretary of the South Wales Coal Owners' Association, and F. M. Witzel, chief secretary of the South Wales and Monmouthshire Joint Committee for Miners' Welfare. The foundation stone was laid by Ramsay MacDonald a year earlier. MacDonald was M.P. for Aberavon and Britain's first Labour Prime Minister. It contained a cinema, billiards room, library and reading room and public hall. It is now the village's only pub, known as the Glyncorrwg.

In July 1902 a dove was seen hovering over the entrance to one of the mines. Considered an evil omen, it led to 300 colliers refusing to work.

Mining ceased in 1970, not before a further influx of workers with developments of council estates.

Described in 1972 by one writer as one of the most dreary and desolate places in Glamorgan, in recent years the valley has been transformed and is now seen as a tourist centre with its rivers and lakes providing good fishing and the mountains and forests ideal for mountain biking, with two world ranked trails, and leisure. New housing on Pleasant view is substantial. There is a bike shop with café, lounge area, open air deck, changing/shower rooms and a bike park together with a Wales Tourist Board rated caravan and camp site.

Glynneath/Glynnedd *Neath Glen*

Glynneath is a large mining village in the beautiful Vale of Neath.

The village's history predates the mining activity however with Rheola Grange recorded as belonging to Gilbert de Clare in 1295. Rheola House was built in the 18th century before being enlarged in the Regency period. The house was purchased by a successful engineer, John Edwards whose nephew was John Nash, the architect of much of Regency London including the redesign of Buckingham Palace. John Edwards' son became a successful solicitor and when extending the house sought designs from his cousin. It appears that Rheola was extended at the same time as Nanteos House in Ceredigion with the involvement of Nash and George Repton. In the 1950s and 60s it was used as an office and training centre for the British

Aluminium Company which helped preserve the property in good condition. The estate is now the subject of plans for a major tourism enterprise designed to conserve the gardens and house.

Aberpergwm House was the 15th century home of Rhys ap Siancyn and came into the hands of the Williams family of Blaen Baglan in 1560. It was remodelled in 1876. During the Second Word War it was used as a school and subsequently as offices by the NCB. It suffered a fire and is in ruins, though it is being maintained by Cadw.

Glynneath stands at the end of the Neath Canal which was completed in 1795. The canal eventually reached Briton Ferry a distance of 13.5 miles. A tramway was built to link the canal with the iron works at Hirwaun and Aberdare with an incline north of Glynneath powered by a Trevithick high pressure steam engine. The canal was eventually connected with the Tennant Canal in 1824 allowing access to the docks at Swansea. Use of the canal continued up to the 1930s and the canal was maintained as a water channel. Parts have now been restored for leisure use.

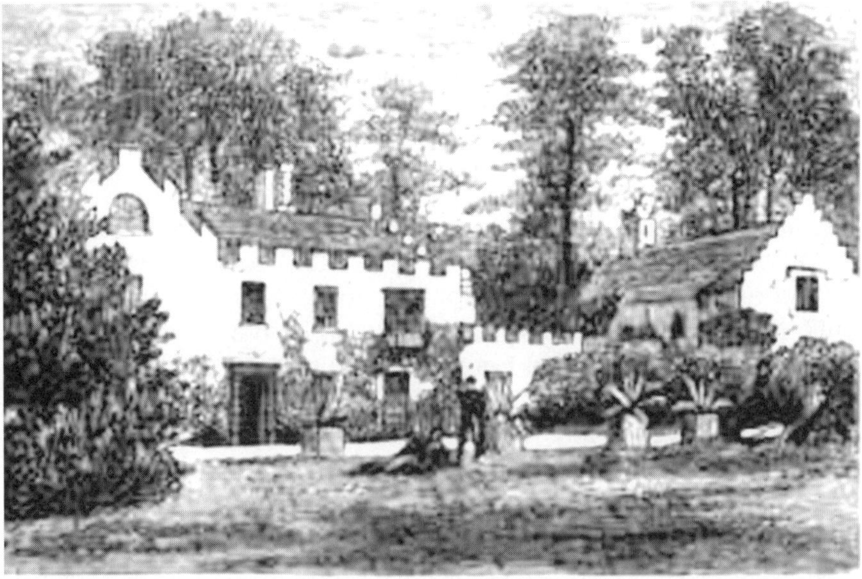

Aberpergwm House , Glyn Neath

Ahead of the canal, there was coal mining in the area and this expanded with the opening of the Rock, Rheola, Pwllfaron, Pentreclwydau, Ladysmith and Aberpergwm collieries. Aberpergwm, closed in the 1980s has been reopened by Energybuild Holdings Ltd. Pentreclwydau was closed in 1967 but new drifts have since opened. It is difficult to estimate the number working in the mines of Glynneath at any one time as over the years pits have closed and others opened or reopened, but at their peak, well over 2000 men were employed.

Glynneath Woollen mill operated in the 19th century and was situated opposite the Lamb and Flag. A medieval corn mill stood at the confluence of the Gwrelych Brook with the River Nedd and belonged to the manor of Miskin.

St Cadoc's Church is situated in the grounds of Aberpergwm House. Originally a chapel of ease to Cadoxton, it is shown on a 16th century map. It was rebuilt in 1808-09 for the Williams family and extended in 1836-41 with the addition of a chancel. The central four panels of the east window are particularly interesting as they come from the cloisters of the former Premonstratensian abbey of Steinfeld in the Eiffel area of Germany and were painted in the mid 16th century. The chapel became a parish church in 1861. It has a western bellcote, south porch and a north vestry. It is Grade II* listed, "for the unusual pre-ecclesiological Gothic interior combining Georgian plaster ceilings with neo-Norman chancel arch and important medieval effigies brought in to enhance the antique effect." (*Source: Cadw)

Other chapels and churches in the village include: Bethany English Presbyterian church built 1858. Bethel Baptist Chapel built 1846. Addoldy Welsh Independent opened 1839. Capel y Glyn, Glyn-Neath Congregational Chapel built 1892. Bethania Calvinistic Methodist built 1906. English Wesleyan Methodist chapel, built 1890. There was also a chapel on Pontneathvaughan Road, now demolished, Peniel a modern Pentecostal hall and St John Kemble Roman Catholic Church.

The Glynneath Welfare Hall and Institute was built between the wars and contained a library and reading room, snooker hall, and cinema. The snooker hall and library were located on the ground floor and cinema. Situated next to the Welfare ground with its tennis courts, playing fields, children's playground, and bowling green. The hall was demolished in the 1990s.

Today Glynneath is a large village by-passed by the A465 Heads of the Valleys dual carriageway. It has a range of banks shops and takeaways as well as pubs and social clubs. There are no large supermarkets though there is a Tesco Express.

In the mid 19th century the village was a tourist destination. The Lamb and Flag was the crest of the Williams family of Aberpergwm and was the name of the local inn. It was at this inn in 1803 that John Hatfield was arrested. A year earlier Hatfield assumed the name of Colonel Hope, the brother of an earl and had committed bigamy by marrying Mary Robinson, the daughter of the landlord of the Fish Inn at Buttermere in the Lake District, and known because of her great beauty as the Maid of Buttermere. The marriage attracted widespread attention and Hatfield was exposed as an impostor, bigamist and forger. He escaped to South Wales where he was eventually apprehended. The story was the subject of Melvyn Bragg's 1987 novel *The Maid of Buttermere* and is also mentioned in Wordsworth's *Prelude*. The Lamb and Flag was described by Leigh in 1835 as a "tolerable inn". Refurbished after a fire in 2008 it continues to offer accommodation.

The Dinas Rock Inn is another old inn whose owner Thomas Morgan advertised "excellent beds and good stabling" as well as "Wines and spirits of superior quality".

Today there are attempts to revive tourism. Above the village on a former opencast mining site is the Walters Arena, used for motor rallying and a stage of the World Rally Championship. To the north is the largest concentration of waterfalls in the United Kingdom and of course there is the canal.

There are the remains of two Wellington bombers in the area. Between Glynneath and Pontneddfecahan the bomber on a night flying exercise crashed after running out of fuel on 19 September, 1939. The second crashed in the mountains above the village on 25 September, 1942.

The local area with its waterfalls is rich in folklore. One story related by Marie Trevelyan in her 1909 book *Folk-lore and Folk-stories of Wales* tells of a man who around sunset rested near a waterfall and saw a water horse emerge from the cascade and stand alongside him. He mounted the horse which took off at a remarkable speed and he noticed that the horse's hooves didn't touch the ground. It was moonrise when he was thrown from the horse and although he had been travelling for just an hour, found himself in Llanddewi Brefi in Ceredigion over 30 miles away as the crow flies. Craig y Llyn was reputed to be the haunt of witches while Wirt Sikes in his book *British Goblins* records that Craig y Ddinas, bears "a distinctly awful reputation as a stronghold of the fairy tribe. Its caves and crevices have been their favourite haunt for many centuries, and upon this rock was held the court of the last fairies who have ever appeared in Wales. Needless to say there are men still living who remember the visits of the fairies to Craig y Ddinas, although they aver the little folk are no longer seen there. It is a common remark that the Methodists drove them away; indeed, there are numberless stories which show the fairies to have been animated, when they were still numerous in Wales, by a cordial antipathy for all dissenting preachers. In this antipathy, it may be here observed, teetotallers were included." While "In the dingle called Cwm Pergwm, in the Vale of Neath, the *Tylwyth Teg* (Fair Folk or fairies) make music behind the waterfall, and when they go off over the mountains the sounds of their harps are heard dying away as they recede."

Glynogwr *Ogmore Glen*

Situated above the Ogwr Fach River, Glynogwr is an ancient village which has seen an increase in population in the last 50 years, but remains a small village. The 1879 map shows just five houses, one being the New Inn which is now a private house.

The village church is built on a traditional Celtic *llan* and was established in the 6th century by St Tyfodwg. The saint's origin is disputed. Some believe he was a Breton pupil of St Illtyd and one of the three saints of Llantrisant (Three Saints Church). Others believe he was a local chieftain, promised sainthood if he and his people converted to Christianity. There is an Ystradyfodwg in the nearby Rhondda valley.

The church dates from the 13th-14th centuries, but was subject to a major renovation in the 1870s by John Prichard and later by G. E. Halliday. Only the tower and parts of the nave are original. Set in the chancel floor is a stone with the image of a pilgrim carrying his staff and purse, with symbols showing his journeys to the Holy Land, Rome and Compostella. It is thought to come from the tomb of a pilgrim who died while travelling through the parish and dates from the 13th or 14th century. It was placed in the chancel floor at the time of Halliday's restoration in 1893.

Glynogwr Calvinistic Methodist Chapel was built in 1819, rebuilt in 1849 and refurbished in 1904-5. It is no longer in use.

Godre'r Graig *The Base of the Rock*

Godre'r Graig is a village in the Swansea valley between Pontardawe and Ystalyfera. The original village developed along Graig Road in part to house workers in the Crimea Colliery, situated to the west of the A4067. The remains of this 19th century colliery can be found in woodland, including the stone built steam pumping engine house, winding engine house and tram road to the canal. The colliery opened in 1854 and closed just eight years later. The Tareni Colliery situated across the valley opened in 1903 and employed up to 947 men but closed in 1949, the then new National Coal Board considering it to be uneconomic.

A new part of the village has developed across the main A4067.

The Swansea Canal which connected Ystradgynlais with Swansea passed through the village and a lock and dry dock remain behind trees opposite the entrance to Graig Newydd, the new part of the village. This was the first in a flight of locks. The canal to Godre'r Graig was opened in 1796 and the section above the village two years later. There was a boat yard at Godre'r Graig which operated until 1918 when it produced its last boat, the *Grace Darling.* In 1871 the canal was purchased by the Great Western Railway and it was run profitably by them until 1895. Over the last 50 years much of the canal has been lost to road development and infill.

The mountain to the west of the village is littered with evidence of disused mine workings and quarries. At the top of Mynydd Allt y Grug is a Bronze Age Cairn, now just one foot high. Also on the mountain are two race tracks used by motorbikes.

Godre'r-Graig Independent Chapel was built in 1909 but is no longer in use as a chapel.

Gorseinon *Einon's Marsh*

Gorseinon was a village until the 19th century when coal mining and tinplate saw a major increase in population. Gorseinon is now a town and outside the scope of this book.

Gowerton *Tregŵyr*

Gowerton, the gateway to north Gower, is a large village with a range of schools including Gowerton Comprehensive School.

It is a relatively modern village, growing up around the Elba Steelworks which were established in 1872. Iron ore was imported from Elba giving the works its title. The Elba Colliery was a drift mine connected to the steelworks by a private railway. It was developed in 1881 but the original drift was closed after an explosion caused the death of 11 miners in 1905. Another drift was opened but closed around 1911. The site of the Elba Steelworks is now a housing estate with the roads bearing the names of Beck and Baldwin, two of the owners of the works over the years.

Prior to 1872 this was a mill village, with the Trafle Corn Mill, and was known as Ffosfelin or Gwter Felin meaning Mill Ditch or Gutter.

St John the Divine's Church was built as a chapel of ease to the parish of Loughor. The land was donated by Sir John Dillwyn Llewelyn of Penllergaer and in 1900 the marble for the interior by Colonel Wright who had established a steelworks in Italy. The marble was brought from Italy together with the craftsmen. The original building was designed by John Fowler of Swansea and Brecon. It has a buttressed west window beneath a double bellcote, with a south porch, nave, chancel and vestry.

Tabernacle Welsh Independent Chapel was built in 1883 and rebuilt in 1893 but is now disused as is Bethel Calvinistic Methodist Chapel which was built in 1873. Bethania Baptist Chapel was established in 1869 and built in 1874 by Thomas Thomas of Llandore. It has since been demolished. Gospel Temple Independent Chapel was built in 1883 and rebuilt in 1899 and is still in use as the United Reformed Church.

Gowerton was once served by two railway stations, with the station on the North Gower line being positioned south of the Commercial Hotel which was built between the two stations. The B4295 was built on the old track. Gowerton Station is now served by the Heart of Wales Line, connecting Swansea Llanelli and Shrewsbury.

There is a range of small shops and takeaways and a Tesco Express mini supermarket.

Goytre *Wood Dwelling*

Goytre is a settlement a little over half a mile north-east of Taibach in Port Talbot. Originally two rows of terraced houses, there was a development of social housing in the 1950s though most dwellings are privately owned.

The village was built for Cwmgwineu Colliery in the Margam Forest. The colliery was established around 1899 but employed fewer than nine men before closing in 1905. It was reopened before 1922 and in 1927 employed 500 men but closed that year. There was a tramway and reservoir serving the colliery.

Hafod Farm, also in the forest was once a grange belonging to Margam Abbey.

St Peter's Church was opened on 31st January, 1915 as a mission church. The corrugated iron building had previously stood in Morfa and was moved at the expense of Miss Emily Charlotte Talbot of Margam. The church was renovated in 2003. There are no other places of worship in Goytre, but there is a large municipal cemetery and a new community centre.

The valley above Goytre is wooded and there is a holiday park offering log cabin and bunkhouse accommodation as well as a licensed restaurant. Walks in the forest include a trip up the valley of Nant Cwmwernderi to a beautifully situated reservoir.

Grovesend

Grovesend is a former mining village north of Gorseinon. The village is named after Grovesend House which, as the name suggests, was approached through a grove of trees along what is now Plas Road. There were a number of collieries including Tirisaf, situated close to Grovesend House and the two Grovesend pits (north and south) to the north of the village. Grovesend Pit opened in 1870 and employed up to 258 men. It closed in 1925. The south pit was situated in the triangle formed by Grove Farm Road while the north was half a mile to the north.

The village has seen some new development and has a school and the Bryn Lliw pub. It had three chapels. Mount Pleasant Independent Chapel was built in 1908. Bethania Baptist Chapel was built in 1908 but has now been demolished and a residential property built on the site. Hebron Independent Chapel was built in 1821, modified in 1849 and again in 1882. It is now a private dwelling.

Gwaun Cae Gurwen

Gwaun Cae Gurwen, locally known as the Waun or GCG is a village on the A474 Ammanford to Pontardawe road. The name is thought to derive from Gwaun Cegerwen, meaning White Hemlock Heath, the heath being the area stretching to the east from the Brynaman road including the rugby pitches. In 1891 there was little to the village other than Mount Pleasant, more recently the site of the Mount Pleasant Inn and houses around the square including the Cae Gurwen Hotel. The area was dominated by engine sheds housing the equipment to haul empty wagons up the incline plain, pulled by the weight of full wagons descending, as although the railway had reached the area, the viaduct allowing trains to travel up from Garnant to GCG wasn't completed till later.

Coal mining started in the village in 1837 with what became known as the 'Old Pit' but mining expanded greatly after the Maerdy pit opened. The colliery was situated north of Tairgwaith and ultimately three pits were worked which by 1945 employed over 2,000 men. All had closed by 1964. In addition to mining, there was the Glynbeudy Tinplate Works, situated off Neuadd Road. It was opened in 1880 and the winding up notice was dated 6th April, 1934.

GCG is not a typical former mining village, being well spread out with green spaces to the north and south-west. The railway line was recently revived as a freight line carrying coal from the opencast mine north-east of Tairgwaith. The village retains a range of small shops and takeaways and has a supermarket, but the array of shops is much smaller today than it was in the 1950s, when the village boasted a railway station, two banks as well as three clubs, pubs and cafés. There is however a revival of the Italian café in the form of Cresci's Café, producing their own ice cream.

Non conformity was the main religious sect with Hermon Independent Chapel built in 1905, Carmel Independent Chapel was built in 1877 and Siloh Calvinistic Methodist Chapel on the corner of Upper Colbren was opened in 1908 but has now been demolished to be replaced by houses.

Photographs of the public conveniences near the level crossing in the village were exhibited at the National Eisteddfod in 1975. The Workmen's Hall and Institute was the largest and most expensive in the area when it was built in 1932 on the site of the former institute that had been built in 1898 from the remains of a Swansea church. The new hall contained a 962 seat cinema and a stage that could house full theatrical performances. It was demolished in 1995 and replaced by the Cwmgors Rugby Clubhouse.

The village has a primary school.

The most famous son of Gwaun Cae Gurwen is Gareth Edwards, said to be he finest scrum half in the history of the game. His name is commemorated in Maes Gareth Edwards, a road off Neuadd Road.

Heol y Cyw *Chicken Street*

Heol y Cyw is a village to the north of Coity. In 1900 there was the disused Raglan Mill, a church, chapel, the Plough Inn and a few houses. There had been small scale coal workings, but the village expanded rapidly over the next twenty years as the Raglan Colliery opened three pits, the first two in 1908, then a third on the site of the former South Glamorgan Colliery. At their peak they employed over 600 men, but all three had closed by 1943, though mining had ceased earlier.

In recent years the village has seen new housing developments, but remains a small village with a school, village shop and the Plough Inn. Heol y Cyw has a large recreation ground and a successful rugby club. It is surrounded by open countryside. Near Ty'n y Waun Farm is the earthwork of an Iron Age hillfort while further north there are the remains of a pillow mound, used for breeding rabbits. Footpaths lead to Blackmill and Glynogwr.

Heol y Cyw had a number of places of worship. St Paul's Church was built in 1889, although services had previously been held in a cottage in the village. A single cell structure, it is unusual in having an eastern porch with the altar at the western end of the church.

Ainon Baptist Chapel on Waun Newydd was built during the early 20th century but had been demolished by 1997. Bethel Independent Chapel was built in 1820, modified in 1829 and again in 1854. New Bethel Independent Chapel was built in 1871 to replace the old chapel which was on the site now occupied by Nant y Coed Close.

Horton

Horton is a small village on the eastern slopes of Port Eynon Bay. The narrow lanes lead down to the beach where there is the Lifeboat Station.

The tiny Horton Wesleyan Methodist Chapel was built in 1872.

There are two caravan parks.

Ilston *Llan Illtyd*

Ilston is a tiny village south-west of Swansea Airport. The stream and woodland make this a pretty village and the 13th century church has a series of 19th century wall paintings. It is thought that the church was built on the site of a simple 6th century monastic cell though the church itself dates from the 13th century. The heavily built tower with its saddleback roof at the south-eastern end of the nave was built over the monastic cell. Two 18th century bells are used while a third bell dating from the 15th century is placed opposite the entrance. Inscribed on this bell is a prayer to St Thomas.

South of the church along the brook are the ruins of the first Baptist Chapel in Wales. It was used after the Reformation in 1660 by John Myles, who had joined the Glasshouse Church in London, an early Particular Baptist congregation, after graduating from Brasenose College Oxford. He was minister at Ilston from 1649 to 1662. When the Restoration imposed the use of the *Book of Common Prayer* on all ministers Myles and his congregation at Ilston left for the Plymouth Colony in America. For a while Myles worked with the Congregationalist church in Rehoboth before he and his congregation were told to leave the area for their Baptist views. They founded the town of Swansea in Massachusetts and the first Baptist Church in America. The land for the new town had been purchased from the Native American tribes but in 1675 the town was attacked and destroyed with the 70 inhabitants surviving in their stockade. Myles took with him to America the *Ilston Book*, a record of the first Baptist church in Wales with a list of all 261 members who came from a wide area of South Wales. The *Ilston Book* is now in the library of Brown's University, Providence, Rhode Island, another community established by a non-conformist Welshman. Alongside the ruins of the chapel are the ruins of Trinity Well, used for baptisms.

Jersey Marine

Jersey Marine is a village three miles east of Swansea. The land was owned by Victor Albert George Child Villiers, 7th Earl of Jersey, who was a prominent 19th century statesman, the principal proprietor of Childs Bank and President of the Welsh Rugby Union 1881-85. He held extensive estates in the Neath and Swansea areas and as a new venture a new resort was planned and the Jersey Marine Hotel was built in 1867. At the time there was no road between the hotel and Crymlyn Burrows and the beach. As part of the complex a tower was built to house a *camera obscura*. In 1892 the Swansea Bay Golf Club was founded adjacent to the hotel and in 1902 the Earl of Jersey opened the clubhouse. The hotel was demolished in 1965 to be replaced by the Towers Hotel and Spa.

To the north of the hotel there were just a few houses and the Burrows Lodge Inn. The hotel was served by the Jersey Marine station on the Great Western Railway and the Tennant Canal passed to the north. Part of the golf course was built on the site of Earlswood Colliery. Crymlyn Burrows Colliery was in use until the 1880s and the site is now used by the Pant y Sais Riding Stables.

600 yards to the west of the village are the ruins of St Margaret's Chapel, a medieval building mentioned in 1291. There was a grange to the north of the chapel and a holy well nearby.

In 1938 an airstrip was built to the south of the golf course as a terminus for Western Airways. There were scheduled services to

Cardiff with connections to Bristol and Weston-Super-Mare. The company operated De Havilland 84 Dragon and De Havilland 89 Rapide aircraft and planned to expand the airport when war intervened. The service had been popular, particularly on Sundays when Welsh pubs were closed.

After the Second World War the Fabian Way dual carriageway was built through Crymlyn Burrows with a connecting road to the village of Jersey Marine. In 1955 the Briton Ferry Bridge was opened, making Fabian Way the primary route into Swansea from the east. The road has seen significant commercial enterprises established including the giant Amazon distribution centre.

The village of Jersey Marine is small, though recently enlarged by the development of housing near the Towers Hotel and at Allt y Grug. There is a good mix of housing in the village which has a primary school, community centre, post office and modern church. There is a petrol service station on Fabian Way.

The road through the village passes over the Tennant Canal and along the Crymlyn Bog Nature Reserve.

South of Fabian Way are the Crymlyn Burrows which are now a Site of Special Scientific Interest. The beach beyond the burrows is frequented by fishermen, horses from the nearby Pant y Sais riding stables, dog walkers and occasionally seals. The beach stretches from the River Neath to the Swansea Docks, a distance of over a mile and the tide recedes for up to a mile. The River Neath had a number of medieval fish traps, designed to trap fish as the tide receded.

Kenfig *Welsh Cynffig meaning Ridge above the Bog*

The village of Kenfig stands between the M4 and the sands of Kenfig Burrows, two and a half miles north of Porthcawl. There is a scattering of houses along the east of the main road with just two small housing developments. There is a visitor centre for the Kenfig National Nature Reserve which covers the dunes to the west and includes Kenfig Pool. South of the village is the Pyle and Kenfig Golf Course which adjoins the dunes.

The dunes hide an important history. Following the Norman Conquest Kenfig was a town of considerable importance. Lewis gives the following history: "This place, which is of considerable antiquity, derives its name from its situation on a ridge of ground above a bog. It was anciently of much greater importance, having formed part of the great lordship of Glamorgan, and passed by right of conquest, with the other possessions of lestyn ab Gwrgan, the last native prince of Glamorgan, to the posterity of Fitzhamon, the Norman invader, in the reign of William Rufus, who, on partitioning the conquered territory among the knights that accompanied him in the expedition, reserved to himself this lordship and castle; and the town, under his descendants and their successors, increased in importance, and was invested with valuable corporate privileges. In the reign of Edward II, these immunities were increased through the influence of this monarch's favourite, the younger Spencer, who obtained for it, in common with other towns in his lordship of Glamorgan, a new charter from the crown. The castle, town, and lordship of Kenvig, about the middle of the fourteenth century, formed part of the dower of the widow of Hugh le Despencer, on her marriage with Guy de Brien. The charter endowing this place with municipal privileges was confirmed by Thomas le Despencer, lord of Glamorgan, in 1360, and renewed by his son Edward, in 1396, and by his daughter Isabel, in 1493.

The decay of the old town, castle, and church are ascribed to an overwhelming inundation of the sea, which took place about the middle of the sixteenth century, and covered with sand an extensive tract in the neighbourhood of the coast. From the desolating effect of this calamitous event the town has never since recovered, and now forms only a small straggling and insignificant village, near the open coast of the Bristol Channel. Kenvig contains about seven hundred and fifty acres of enclosed land, and eight hundred acres of waste, which latter are principally composed of sandbanks and rabbit warrens, of about twelve miles in extent, from Skeir rocks to Briton Ferry. These sandbanks, subsequently to the inundation, have been planted with the *arundo arenaria*, in order to bind them; and, on taking a farm on the adjoining moor, the tenant usually covenants in his lease to give annually the labour of a day or more, in proportion to the extent of his farm, for planting it. The bog referred to in the etymology of the name of this place has, from, time immemorial, formed a lake, which is nearly two miles in circumference, and, though situated close to the sea-shore, and encompassed with sand, never imbibes any muriatic properties. Prior to the desolation caused by the furious encroachment of the sea, the road from Cardiff to Swansea and Carmarthen passed through the town; but it was subsequently diverted through Pyle, and now passes at the distance of about a mile and a half to the north of it. The borough still retains its municipal privileges, and is governed by a portreeve, recorder, and aldermen, of whom the portreeve is annually chosen from among the in-dwelling, or resident burgesses, subject to the approbation of the constable of the castle… The town-hall, of which the lower part has been converted into a public-house, was built, about the commencement of the present century, at an expense of £400. Two fairs were formerly held here annually; the first commenced on Whit-Tuesday, and the second on the eve of St. James the Apostle, and each continued eight days." (*A Topographical Dictionary of Wales* 1833)

The remnants of the great medieval fortress of Kenfig Castle stand to the north of the dunes between Ffynnon Lygad and the M4, south of the Cynffig River and the Kenfig Industrial estate. It was circular with a tall 45 foot square tower and hall. In 1300 a gatehouse facing the town was added. Some 300 yards to the south lay the church of St James which was abandoned to the sands sometime around 1400. The walled borough of Kenfig stood between the church and the castle positioned at the northern angle. Some foundations are visible in the sands. The borough was eventually abolished in 1883.

Finds of Roman artefacts have led to the belief that there was a Roman fort situated near the site of the old town, alongside the road and guarding the crossing of the river which would have been a wide estuary at the time.

The town hall referred to by Lewis is now the Prince of Wales Hotel. Originally the guildhall was built on pillars at the beginning of the 17th century but rebuilt in 1808 with the public house occupying the ground floor. Meetings continued in the upper chamber.

The dunes offer extensive walks. There are boardwalks to the bird hides around Kenfig Pool but otherwise paths are of sand with some a little boggy after wet weather. Beyond the dunes lies the peaceful beach of Kenfig Sands.

To the south of the beach lies Sker House, a 16th century mansion built on the site of a former monastic grange. Altered in the 18th and

19th centuries, it was restored at the turn of the millennium by the Buildings at Risk Trust. The project led to an overspend and the property was purchased by the historian and biographer Niall Fergusson. The house was the inspiration for R. D. Blackmore's novel *The Maid of Sker*, 1872. In the 16th and 17th centuries the house was the home of a branch of the Turberville family who were staunch Roman Catholics and members of the household were imprisoned for recusancy. It was recorded that in 1598 fourteen prisoners died at Cardiff prison, one being "James Turbervill of Newton Nottage, gentleman, committed for recusancy".

Kenfig Hill

Kenfig Hill is a village between Pyle and Cefn Cribwr five miles north-west of Bridgend. The village began as a mining village for the coal mines to the north-east of the village, but the Bryn Du Coke Ovens were also a major employer although these had closed by 1900. The Maesteg to Porthcawl railway ran to the north of the village as did a tramway.

With its proximity to the M4, Kenfig Hill today is a good commuting village with new houses. There are also industrial estates in the surrounding area.

The village has a primary and comprehensive school and a range of shops and banks. The 1930s cinema is now a supermarket.

The building of St Theodore's Church began in 1889 when Miss Emily Talbot of Margam Park laid the foundation stone and was completed in 1891. It was built in memory of Miss Talbot's brother, Theodore, who had died following a hunting accident in 1876. The church was designed by Halliday and Anderson, with the south aisle, extended nave, vestry and heating chamber added in 1909 by Cook and Edwards of Bridgend. It became a parish church in 1923. It has a western bellcote topped with a mini spire with a clock incorporated into the structure.

Elim Independent Chapel was built in 1847, and rebuilt in 1880. It closed in 1993 and was demolished in 1995. Rehoboth Apostolic Church in Evans Street has been demolished. Moriah Calvinistic Methodist Chapel was built in 1850 and Moriah Place named after it. The chapel has been demolished. St David's Presbyterian Church was built in 1928 and is still in use. Bethel Mission Chapel and the Wesleyan Methodist chapel have both been demolished.

In fields south of the High Street is Pen y Castell, an Iron Age defended enclosure with double banks and ditches adjacent to the electricity pylons.

Killay

Killay today is a busy, popular suburb of Swansea on high ground three and a half miles west of the city. Morgan attributes the name to a corruption of Cil Fai, meaning an isolated plain, though the Welsh spelling is Cilâ.

In 1879 the village consisted of just a few houses, the Commercial Inn, The Black Boy public house and Siloan Welsh Baptist Chapel, all of which remain, though Siloan was rebuilt in 1898. The area to the north of Gower Road was farmland, while to the south was woodland. By 1900 Killay House had been built and Rhydydefed Colliery was operational in Clyne Woods. By 1918 there were more houses along Gower Road and Rhydydefed Colliery had closed. It was only after 1945 that the village saw major expansion in housing. Today there is a shopping centre with its own pub, the Village Inn. Killay House is now a National Children's Home. The church of St Hilary was built in 1926 to plans by the Swansea architect Glendinning Moxham.

Kittle

Kittle is a hamlet on the Gower, to the east of Pennard. It has expanded in recent years and has a village hall, some shops and the Beaufort Arms. A pleasant settlement with a green and new housing to the north and south of the B4436, Kittle was previously surrounded by quarries. Great Kittle House to the south of the village dates from the 16th century.

Knelston

Knelston is a small village on the A4118 a mile south-west of Reynoldston in the Gower. There was a 12th century church, Llan y Tayre Mayre or the church of the Three Marys. It was later dedicated to St Maurice and St Mary, but was in a state of ruin by the 17th century though burials continued for another century. The ruins lie between the school and Knelston Hall Farm. To the north of the church site is Burry Menhir, a seven foot standing stone of uncertain date, but recorded in 1784 as being one of four stones.

Providence Baptist Chapel was built in 1858 and together with the manse is now used as holiday accommodation. There is a small caravan park in the village.

Laleston

According to Samuel Lewis the village "derives its name from Lalys, a native of Palestine, and an eminent architect, whom Richard de Granville brought over with him on his return from the Holy Land, and employed to build the abbey of Neath in this county. As a reward for the ability which he displayed in the erection of that magnificent structure, Richard bestowed on him this manor, to which he gave his name, and on which he resided, until, after erecting several churches and castles in the principality, he was appointed architect to Henry I, and removed to London." De Granville had gone on a pilgrimage to Palestine in 1111 and as well as Neath Abbey, Lalys built the tower of St Illtyd's Church on Newcastle Hill, Bridgend.

The old village of Laleston was the centre for quarrying and a limited amount of coal mining was carried on in the parish. Today it is a dormitory village for Bridgend which lies two miles east. The village has expanded greatly in recent years but there are some interesting older properties.

St David's Church dates from the 13th century and was refurbished by John Prichard in 1871. It is Grade I Listed with its tower, nave with waggon roof and chancel. In the churchyard is a preaching cross some 11 foot high.

Horeb Calvinistic Methodist Chapel was built in 1831 and modified in 1852 with the addition of a schoolroom and house. It is no longer used as a chapel, but as a private school. Bethel Baptist Chapel was built in 1848.

Laleston House the home of the Bennet family in the 18th and 19th centuries has been demolished to make way for modern housing. In

December 1769 Henry Knight Esquire of Laleston challenged Thomas Bennet Esquire of Laleston House to a duel, issuing the following challenge:

> "Respect to the Company prevented my taking the Proper Notice of the Insolence of your Language yesterday at Ewenny, but it were Disrespect to myself not to resent it now. I therefore acquaint your self-Importance that you behaved like a Fool and spoke like a Liar – which I am ready to make good as a Gentleman ought, when and wheresoever you think proper to appoint."
> Hen: Knight.Tythegston, Dec. 30th 1769

The Laleston Inn was formerly the Laleston Country Club, as a way of circumventing licensing laws. The building dates from 1600 and a fragment of an incised floriated cross was discovered at the base of a ground floor window.

The Oystercatcher Inn on the main road dates from the 16th century, but despite being Grade II listed as a characteristic village inn, it is now closed with plans for conversion.

Ty Mawr or The Great House Hotel, again on the main road, dates from the late 16th to early 17th century and was formerly owned by Margam Abbey.

In addition to the Laleston Inn and the Great House there is the Mackworth Arms and the Braseria El Prado.

The village has a primary school and a small shopping area.

Landimore

Landimore is a hamlet on the north coast of Gower a mile east of Cheriton. There are signs that it was once a much larger village and it is thought that the church at Cheriton was originally established here. The hamlet overlooks the salt marsh which is owned by the National Trust.

On 14th August, 1440 the crusader Hugh Jonys, was knighted at Jerusalem and subsequently became the Knight Marshall of England. On his retirement he was granted the manor fee of Landimor by John, Duke of Norfolk who was Lord of Gower at the time. Sir Hugh built a mansion there around 1451 at what is now Bovehill Farm. The house was abandoned after 50 years and only a few walls remain. It is known as Bovehill or Landimore Castle. The position of Knight Marshal meant that Sir Hugh was authorized to hear and determine all pleas of the Crown. His court was called the Court of Marshalsea.

Three quarters of a mile east of Landimore is Weobley Castle, now under the care of Cadw. Built at the beginning of the 14th century by David De la Bere, steward to De Braose Lord of Gower, the castle is set in an imposing position on the limestone overlooking Llanrhidian Marsh. Although in outline a castle, it was built more for comfort than defence and was occupied by the De la Bere family well into the 15th century. David's nephew John inherited the estate and married into the De Turberville family. His second son was Sir Richard De la Bere who was knighted at the Battle of Crècy in 1346 and was known to be a friend of the Black Prince.

The castle passed into the hands of Sir Rhys ap Thomas, the supporter of Henry VII, and, over the years, the Herbert and Mansel families.

Lewistown

Lewistown is a village in the Ogmore Valley, just south of Ogmore Vale. It was named after the Lewis Merthyr Company. It grew up in the first twenty years of the 20th century with the opening of two quarries on Craig Pentre-beili when Pentre-beili terrace was built. Llangeinor Terrace followed together with limited development along the main road. In more recent years there have been housing developments on both sides of Blackmill Road.

The village has no shop, or place of worship but there is a rugby club.

In 1914 the Lewis Merthyr Coal Company opened the Catherine and Anne pits as the Rhondda Main Collieries. They operated until 1924 employing over 1,000 men at their peak. After closure, the site became a coal washery.

Llandarcy

Llandarcy was the site of Britain's first major oil refinery, opened in 1920 by the Anglo Persian Oil Company, later British Petroleum. A garden village was built to house workers from the refinery and has a consistency of style with plenty of open spaces. There is one large mock black and white timber house and a village hall, but no place of religion or public house. The village was named after the founder of the company, William Knox D'Arcy. The oil refinery which employed up to 2,600 men closed in 1998 and the site is to form the new village of Coed Darcy.

On the green between The Greenway and Prettyman Drive was a circular enclosure visible as a cropmark from the air and used by local children in the 1920s as the site of a maypole and children dancing. 150 yards due east of the village hall is a prehistoric cairn of uncertain age.

Llanddewi

Llanddewi is a tiny village two miles west of Reynoldston. Archaeological finds show that the area was inhabited in the Neolithic and Bronze Ages. The church of St David was built in the early 14th century by Henry de Gower, Bishop of St David's who also built a palace in the village. The palace was abandoned shortly after construction due to a lack of a water supply.

The church has a weeping chancel and a tower with saddleback roof. The bell which dates from 1781 is said to be the largest and loudest in Gower. The church was restored in 1876 and 1905. There is a sundial on the church wall.

Llanddewi Castle Farm dates from the 16th century and is thought to have been built on the site of the former Bishop's Palace, which may have been fortified.

Llangeinor

Llangeinor today is effectively two villages. The old village is tiny, centred around the church of St Cein on a ridge between the valleys of the Garw and Ogmore six miles north of Bridgend. The 19th and 20th century village is situated in the Garw valley.

St Cein was one of the fifteen daughters of King Brychan after whom Brecon is named. Born in 451AD Cein devoted herself to a religious life and rather than marry a local prince, left for Somerset where she

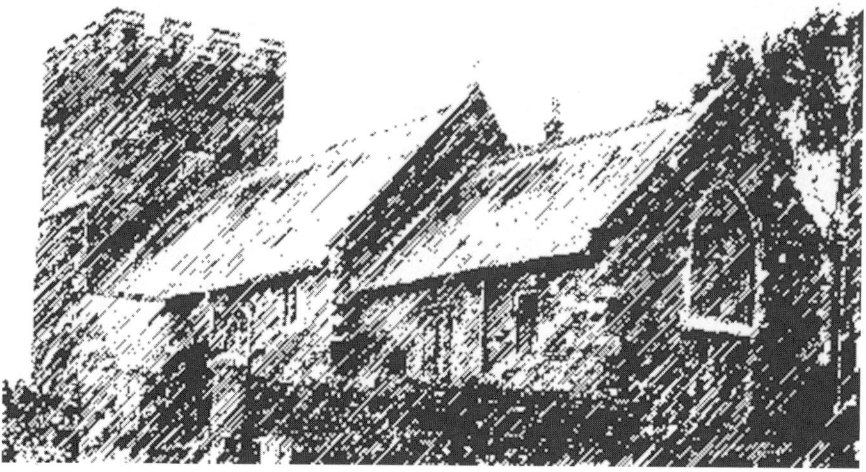

St Cein's Church

founded a religious community at Keynsham between Bath and Bristol. She also visited Cornwall where she established the church at St Keyne before returning to Wales at the suggestion of her nephew, St Cadoc. She established a community at what became Llangeinor where she died a virgin in 505AD and was buried on Llangeinor Mountain.

The church of St Cein dates from 1180 and retains much of its original fabric although heavily restored in 1894. There is a nave, chancel and west tower with a south porch. In the north of the churchyard there is a raised area said to contain the bodies of men from Brecon slain in a battle which took place some two miles north of the village on Mynydd Llangeinor. They had disturbed the Michaelmas Fair in Bridgend and killed one Jenkin Mathew. Their bodies were transported to the church by oxen and were buried in a heap.

Opposite the church was a monastic grange belonging to Margam Abbey, though forfeited in 1337. The parish poor house was also situated opposite the church. It predated the Poor Laws, having been an ancient court-house, later called a church-house appropriated for the residence of paupers. The 1841 census lists three paupers in residence, aged 55, 80 and 85.

The Llangeinor Arms has been in existence since the middle of the 19th century. This part of the village is now a conservation area.

In the 19th and 20th centuries development took place in the Garw valley. There is evidence of small scale quarrying and at least one trial mine, but the main coal mining activity was further up the valley. 19th century developments in the village remained small scale with the Green Meadow Inn. In 1924 the Calfaria Baptist Chapel was built in the valley below the main road.

20th century development has taken place to the south with a large 1950s and 60s social housing estate built above the main road. Attractive new housing has been built on Heol Ty Nant, taking advantage of the views afforded by the mountain.

There is a primary school and a factory, Airborne Systems, and a post office. On the valley floor is the sports ground.

Above the 19th century village stands Tynton Farmhouse, the birthplace of Dr Richard Price (1723-1791). Price, the son of a local dissenting minister was a mathematician and moral philosopher. He was a minister at Newington Green Unitarian Church and was prominent in political circles. He was a major influence on the American Revolution, with Benjamin Franklin, Thomas Jefferson, Thomas Paine and John Adams, who later became the second president of the United States, among his visitors. He was invited to America to assist in the financial administration of the new country but refused to leave Britain. He was acquainted with Pitt the Younger, Joseph Priestley, Adam Smith and David Hume and amongst his congregation was Mary Wollstonecraft, the campaigner for women's rights and mother of Mary Shelley, author of *Frankenstein.* He was offered the post of private secretary to Lord Shelburne, the British Prime Minister, in 1782.

Llangennith

Llangennith is a picturesque village on the north-western tip of the Gower Peninsular. Named after the church dedicated to St Cennydd, who founded the church here in the 6th century, there was once a priory here and the farm buildings which still attach to the church were part of the monastic buildings. The present church dates from 1102 and is in a traditional Celtic *llan.* It has a weeping chancel and a tower unusually placed at the north-east corner of the nave. It is also very large and of a high quality with a saddleback roof. Inside there is the damaged effigy of a De la Mare knight. The farm next to the church is known as the 'College', signifying that it was once part of the monastic settlement. Rees gives the following history "a priory founded by Roger Earl of Warwick in the reign of King Stephen, and annexed to the abbey of St. Taurinus at Evreux in Normandy. It was seized as an alien priory, and granted by Henry the sixth in 1441 to All Souls College, Oxford."

St Cennydd was, according to legend, the son of the Dihoc, Prince of Letavia. Dihoc had been summoned to attend King Arthur for Christmas in Gower and while there a woman who accompanied him gave birth to a son Cennydd, the result of incest. Cennydd was born a cripple with the calf of one leg attached to the thigh. Dihoc ordered the child to be tossed in the River Loughor but before this was done a priest baptized him. The child was placed in a woven osier cradle and set adrift. When the cradle reached the sea a storm arose and carried the baby to the isle of Inisweryn, thought to be Worm's Head. A flock of seagulls picked up the child using their beaks and claws and carried him to safety, preparing a bed for him from their breast feathers. The birds protected the child from the wind, rain and snow by extending their wings. Sabine Baring-Gould continues the story: "Before nine days had passed, an angel descended from heaven, bearing a brazen bell, which he applied to the mouth of the infant, who sucked vigorously at the handle, and received therefrom much satisfaction.

Thus Keneth lived till he was able to walk, and the garments in which he had been wrapped when exposed, grew with him, expanding, as does the bark of a tree. One day, a peasant who lived near the sea, and who had no family, happening to light on the child, took it up and carried it home, and committed it to his wife, who at once put the little Keneth to bed. This caused tremendous excitement among the gulls; they came in vast numbers, and dividing into two bands, one entered the house and pulled the coverlet off the sleeping child, and the other, with screams and by the aid of beak and claw, drove the cattle of the husbandman towards the sea. The man, alarmed for his live-stock, hastily carried back Keneth to where he had found him, whereupon the gulls drove back his cattle to their pastures, and, in the most tidy manner, replaced the coverlet whence they had plucked it. And now daily a female stag came out of the forest, and squirted her milk into the bell that Keneth employed as his feeding-bottle, and likewise filled some hollows in the rocks hard by. Living thus, on milk and roots and herbs, Keneth grew to the age of eighteen, and received instruction in Scripture and the Articles of the Faith from an angel. Then this heavenly teacher informed him he must depart to a reedy spot about a mile distant." It is thought that St Cennydd established his hermitage on Burry Holms, the islet at the northern tip of Rhossili Bay. Baring-Gould gives further information on St Cennydd, "It fell out that David, Teilo and Padarn were on their way, summoning the abbots and bishops of Wales to the Council of Llanddewi Brefi, and were hospitably received by Keneth. David requested him to attend the synod. Observe my leg, I am a cripple, how can I go? answered Keneth. Then David prayed, and Keneth's contracted leg was relaxed, so that he could walk as any other man. This did not please Keneth, and he prayed, and at once up went his limb as before and the calf once again"

Other less colourful sources suggest he was the son of Gildas, a married man, and was a student at Llantwit Major and appointed by St David to establish Christianity in Gower. He is also remembered at Broweroc and Poumelin in Brittany where he is depicted in a statue.

His son was Ufelwy, who became Bishop of Llandaff, and according to Welsh tradition was one of those who met St Augustine and rejected his overtures to adopt Roman Catholicism.

Opposite the church, across the village green, is the King's Head.

To the west of the village is Burry Holms Island, accessible at low tide. On the island there is a Bronze Age cairn and remains of an Iron Age promontory fort and a monastery.

On the stream that flows south of the village were two corn mills and there are a number of lime kilns scattered around the vicinity as are a prehistoric hut circle site and Iron Age hillforts at Harding Down.

Llangennith Methodist Chapel was built in 1863 and Zion Methodist Chapel was built in 1867. Neither appears to be in current use.

In the last 40 years the village has expanded with modern houses and bungalows, but the village has retained its character. The beach is particularly popular with surfers and there is a surf shop near the church. There are a number of camping and caravan sites.

Llangewydd

Llangewydd is a hamlet two miles west of Pen-y-fai, south of the M4, consisting of just Llangewydd Hall and Court Farm together with a few cottages. It takes its name from St Cewydd, the son of the Pictish King Caw of Prydyn, who studied under St Cadog at Llancarfan in the 6th century. His church at Llangewydd is lost, but thought to have been on a crossroads south-east of Llangewydd Court Farm where there is a rectangular building platform. It is thought that any existing settlement connected with the church was displaced when Llangewi Grange was granted to Margam Abbey in 1153. There are remains of Llanguig Court which replaced the grange buildings in the grounds of Llangewydd Court. There was a castle at Llangewydd, destroyed in the early 13th century. Again the site is uncertain, but thought to be to the south of Llangewydd.

Llanguicke *Llangiwg*

Situated on an old pilgrim route a mile due north of Pontardawe lies the ancient little church of Llangiwg. The parish once covered a large area. St Ciwg was a 6th century saint, said to be the son of Arawn, one of the three counselling knights of King Arthur. Little remains of the Norman church which replaced the Celtic church following an extensive restoration in 1812, but there are a number of interesting features including the top of a 7th-9th century stone cross, a water stoup in the porch and the lepers' window in the east wall. The graveyard accepted the burial of victims of the 1866 cholera epidemic which had been refused in the towns and villages. It was also the final resting place for residents of the Pontardawe Workhouse. The squat church tower was lowered during the restoration as it was leaning. The church was purchased by the Friends of Llangiwg in 2007 following its closure in 2004. In 2010 a new window by the artist Marilyn Griffiths was installed. In the churchyard is a holy well. The 19th century gates incorporate an iron kissing gate.

Beside the church once stood the stone built curate's house which later became the Cilybebyll Arms and later still the Maendy Arms, before abandonment in the 19th century.

Llangyfelach

Llangyfelach today is a commuter village three and a half miles north of Swansea city centre, bordering the M4. It owes its existence to a monastery set up by St David and the church is dedicated to St David and St Cyfelach, the latter believed to have been Bishop of Llandaff from 880 to 927. The oldest part of the village around the church makes an attractive setting, with the Plough and Harrow inn and village green.

The medieval church was destroyed in a storm in 1803, leaving only the tower intact. A new church was constructed on the site of a tithe barn to the north of the former church in 1830-33 by T. Griffiths. Further work was carried out in 1913-14 by W. D. Caroe. The church consists of a nave, chancel, vestry and south porch. Stained glass in the church is 20th century, with the east window by Kempe depicting the Crucifixion with the Virgin Mary and St John.

The tower which shows some signs of restoration, has a lintel to the northern door formed by a slab with incised framed ring cross dating from the 9th century. South of the tower is the socketed base of a pillar cross.

Nepotism showed itself among the local clergy as Carlisle records in his 1811 *Topographical Dictionary of the Dominion of Wales*: "It is rather a singular circumstance, that the present Curate is both Curate and Clerk of the Parish. As the Salary of the Clerk amounts to about £100. per annum, and the nomination being with the Vicar, the Father of the present Curate, he nominated his Son (The Rev. William Davies), who afterwards became Curate. He appoints a person to perform the common offices of a Clerk, for which he receives the fees; but the Curate receives the bulk of the Salary, which arises from Easter Offerings."

In the late 19th century the village was the scene of coal mining, with the Cefngyfelach Colliery operational in 1888 but abandoned by 1916. The Tir Ffordd Colliery, situated to the north of the village was operating in 1935 but closed after the Second World War.

In 1956 the Steel Company of Wales established the Velindre Tin Plate Works to the north of the village. It operated until 1989 and the site was cleared in 1995 and used for the National Eisteddfod in 2006. Llangyfelach has grown in the last 50 years with new housing. The village has a primary school and village shop. Bethel Calvinistic Methodist Chapel was built in 1809, rebuilt in 1847 and 1865.

For the future, there are plans for a golf course and housing to the west of the village and for a business park and urban village to the north of the M4.

Llangynwyd

Old Llangynwyd is an unspoilt hill village two miles south of Maesteg. The name is derived by the dedication of the church to St Cynwyd, but Baring-Gould casts doubt on Cynwyd having established the church. According to Baring-Gould, "Cynwyd Cynwydion was the son of Cynfelyn ab Arthwys, of the race of Coel Godebog, and the father of Clydno Eiddyn, Cynan Genhir, Cynfelyn Drwsgl, and Cadrod Calchfynydd. But he was one of the "Men of the North," who were all warriors, and there is no proof that he was ever connected with Glamorgan. Like the rest of those northern chieftains, he has been appropriated by the compilers of the late Achau'r Saint (Ancestry of the Saints) in the Iolo MSS., and made to be a Saint of Bangor Catwg, at Llancarfan. The only evidence that seems to support Cynwyd's

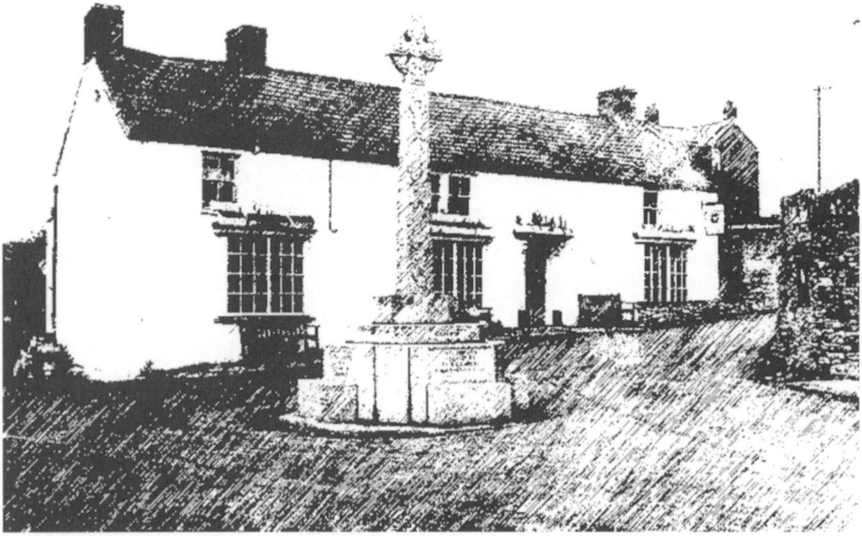

Llangynwyd Memorial and Corner House Inn

association with Llangynwyd. is the fact that two of the largest farms in the Middle Hamlet, Bryn Cynan and Maes Cadrod, contain the names of two of his sons. Browne Willis gives Llangynwyd as dedicated to S. Cunetus, that is, Cynwyd, with festival on September 23. Edward Lhuyd gives as well October 15 as the festival day. Ffynnon Gynwyd is near the church. The old day-school, which stood near the church tower, was called by the villagers Ty Cynwyd; and there was formerly near the village a cromlech popularly called "the Old Church"."

Whoever the founder, the church was established in the 6th century. The present church dates from the 13th century with a 15th century tower, both renovated in the 1892 by G. E. Halliday and financed by Miss Olive Talbot of Margam Abbey. The 10th Century stone socket of a Celtic Cross is to be found in the porch wall and the 19th century renovation revealed wall paintings of Moses and Aaron and a fragment of a painted rood screen. In the Chancel is the grave of Ann Thomas, the Maid of Cefn Ydfa, marked by a brass plate, while the grave of her lover Wil Hopcyn, the bard, is marked beneath the Yew Tree outside. (For the story of these lovers see Coytrahen)

Bethesda Welsh Independent Chapel was built as part of a terrace of cottages in 1795. It has sadly been modernized and converted into a dwelling. The same fate has met Babell Welsh Wesleyan Methodist Chapel a little further along Llan Road.

There are two hostelries in the village, the Old House and the Corner House. The Old House traces its origins to 1147, but the building dates from the 17th century with 18th and 19th century additions. It has the only thatched roof in the Llynfi valley and is a popular tourist attraction as is the Corner House. This building dates back to 1722, the lower half having being the old Tithe Barn, Originally three cottages, one of which was occupied by Wil Hopcyn. It appears to have become a beer house in the 1840s. On 24th September, 1873, Fanny Rees the landlord's wife was found hanged in the house with a verdict of suicide while in an unsound state of mind. In 1922 the police tried to close the pub, which is somewhat ironic in that during my time in the area it was the venue for the police choir on a Friday night. It was not until 1966 that a full licence was granted. The Corner House today is a popular pub and restaurant. The pub is said to be haunted by the ghost of a man, possibly a Cromwellian trooper.

The village still celebrates the New Year with the custom of Mari Lwyd or the Grey Mare, with a horse's skull (traditionally a mare's) draped in a white sheet and flowers paraded around the village by a group, hoping to get refreshments at each house.

Malkin relates that the ill-fated Edward II is said to have found a temporary refuge at a farm named Gelli Lenore in 1326 before being captured and murdered at Berkeley Castle in 1327. Baring-Gould however gives the following account of the King's escape from Caerphilly Castle:

"We must remember that for what follows we have only local legend. Edward, disguised as a peasant, escaped to the parish of Llangynwyd, about twenty miles distant, where he is said to have hired himself as a cowherd to a farmer, who retained him only a few days and then, finding him an awkward fellow, dismissed him. The King, according to another tradition, concealed himself all day in the branches of an oak tree near the house, and retired to the farm buildings for the night. The old tree stood till some years ago, and went by the name of Cadair Edward (Edward's Chair). However, what appears to be the truth is that Edward did effect his escape and reached Margam on November 3rd and thence to Neath, where he met Rhys ab Gruffydd, Lord of Dynevor, who informed him that he had no chance of gaining adherents in Wales."

Court records tell us that in 1576, one "Jane vergh Thomas, formerly of Llangonoyd," was in court "for petty larceny. Judgment, that she be placed in the stocks for two hours in Cardiff market."

Below the village are the remains of Llangynwyd Castle, built on a spur between Nant y Castell and Nant Caelloi. The motte and bailey castle of the 12th century was first mentioned in 1246. The castle was destroyed in 1257 and rebuilt by Gilbert de Clare in the 1260s. This building was contemporaneous with de Clare's building of Caerphilly Castle and the gatehouse resembled the inner eastern gatehouse at Caerphilly. The castle was destroyed in 1294-5 and never rebuilt. This once splendid medieval fortress is now reduced to piles of stone and earthworks, partly concealed in woodland.

A little over a mile west of the village is the impressive Iron Age hillfort of Y Bwlwarcau. The inner enclosure is well defined with ramparts and ditches with a much larger outer enclosure of 10 acres with two widely spaced ramparts. Aerial photographs show considerable damage caused by vehicles in the last ten years. East of the hillfort is a group of some 13 cairns of uncertain date. The area is accessible by a footpath leading from Waun y Gilfach.

In the Llynfi valley three quarters of a mile east of the old village is the modern part of Llangynwyd and the hamlet of Pont Rhyd y Cyff. Here there is a primary school and comprehensive school, a housing estate and a small parade of shops and a service station. The main road has a mixture of housing while to the east down Station Road is The Railway Inn. Further along was the Tyler's Arms, now closed. The Tyler's had an attractive setting on the banks of the River Llynfi and beyond it a collection of pretty cottages and modern houses set amongst trees. Pont Rhyd y Cyff Corn Mill was the last corn mill in the valley and was operational into the 20th century. It has been converted into private accommodation but it retains much of its machinery which has been partially restored to working order. It has an iron overshot waterwheel 10 feet in diameter.

Ainon Welsh Baptist Chapel in Station Road was built in 1925. Moriah Calvinistic Methodist Chapel in Station Road was built in 1876 by the architect Mr Gray of Llangollen. The modern Shiloh Apostolic Church is on Llan Road. On the corner of Station Road and Bridgend Road stands the old National School. By 1940 this had become a mission church known as St Stephens, though it now appears to be defunct.

Llanmadoc

The village is named after its church dedicated to St Madoc, a 6th century saint who Baring-Gould equates with Aidan son of Gildas. Baring-Gould gives the following information: "The Gwyl Mabsant, or Patronal Festival, is observed at Llanmadoc on November 12. One feature of it was, and is still, a particular sort of pie, made of chopped mutton and currants. According to an old Gower custom, every farmer endeavoured to sow his wheat on or before Llanmadoc Mabsant, for the old people used to say that whatever was sown after then would lie in the ground forty days before it began to spring."

Llanmadoc is an attractive village in north-west Gower overlooking Whiteford Sands.

The church is 13th century though there is a 5th-6th century inscribed stone set in a window sill, which reads 'Advenctus filius Guanus'. There is a crenellated tower with a saddleback roof, nave and chancel with a south porch. The altar font was carved by Revd J. D. Davies the incumbent and Gower historian who also oversaw a refurbishment in 1865. Davies was also responsible for the alpine styled Old Rectory opposite the church.

On Llanmadoc Hill south of the village is the Bulwark Iron Age hillfort and to the west the remains of a large number of cairns that have been robbed over the years. Baring-Gould relates: "There is an interesting encampment called the Bulwarks in Llanmadoc parish on a hill-top, where bronze Celts have been found. The people have a legend about it, that a bloody battle was fought between the men holding this fort and another body of men on Arsin Down, that Tankin was the name of the leader of the men on Llanmadoc Hill, and that he was slain, and "they fought till they were over their boots in blood." The dead were buried in the mounds that strew the moor." He also tells that "during the incumbency of the Rev. Watkin Knight, who was rector of the parish 1773-98, a maid, in trying to light the kitchen fire one morning, found the smoke pouring into the room, and she jokingly remarked, "There must be a man in the chimney!" And a man was actually found there, smothered, stuck fast. The men who pulled the body out on to the thatched roof of the rectory shouted down to Mr. Knight whether they should put a noose round his neck and lower him thus or roll him down. "Roll him down," said Mr. Knight, and the body flopped at his feet. A consultation was held. It was decided that it was the corpse of a would-be thief, and so it was carried up the hill and buried in the midst of the ancient camp."

To the west of Llanmadoc is Broughton Bay, Baring-Gould again: "A sad occurrence took place in Broughton Bay on the night of January 27th, 1868. Eighteen vessels bound from Llanelly had left the port, unaware of a heavy ground sea that was running. On reaching Whitford Lighthouse two anchored, the rest stood out into the open, when the wind on which they relied died away; the flood tide set in against them. The result was that they drifted helplessly, some against the rocks, some against each other; and in all sixteen vessels were totally lost, and most of their crews perished. This happened during the night, and in the morning from Whitford Sker to Burry Holms the shore was strewn with seamen's clothes, broken spars, shattered hulls of stranded vessels, sails, carpenters' tools, vast quantities of coal, and corpses.

A remarkable and somewhat mysterious occurrence took place in connection with this wreck. The circumstance is related by the Rev. J. D. Davies, rector of the parish. The choir happened on that evening to be practising in the church, "When suddenly an indescribable scream of terror was heard in the churchyard, as of one in the last extremity of mortal fear. I immediately ran out to see what was the matter, and saw a young lad, whom I knew very well, standing in the middle of the walk, not far from the porch, with his face not only blanched, but actually distorted with fright. "What is the matter, my lad?" I asked. "Oh !" he replied, "I saw a man without his hat come and look in through the window." I brought the poor terrified lad into the church, where he remained some little time before he came to himself. It was currently believed that what he saw was the apparition of one of the poor seamen who was drowned, as it was just about the time when the wreck took place.""

The village has a shop and the Britannia Inn at Cheriton stands just to the east.

Llanmorlais

Situated in north-east Gower south of Crofty, Llanmorlais was shown on pre-1900 maps as Glan-morlais and means Banks of the Morlais River. The Glan-morlais Colliery was at the end of the railway to Killay and Swansea which closed in 1931. The village consists of Station Road which has some older terraced cottages and farm buildings but most of the housing is modern. Tirzah Baptist Chapel dates from 1905. The Morlais River flows to the north of Station Road and enters the sea through Salthouse Pill.

Llanrhidian

Llanrhidian is an attractive north Gower village built on a slope overlooking Llanrhidian Sands and Marsh and the Loughor estuary. It takes its name from the church dedicated to St Rhidian and St Illtyd. Rhidian was a 6th century Celtic Saint who some believe was St Illtyd's wife while others relate a story that he was a pupil of St Cennydd and went on a pilgrimage to St David's bringing back a flame from the shrine of St David.

The church was granted by William de Turberville of Coity Castle in about 1167 to the Knights Hospitallers of St John, who were responsible for beginning the building of the present church in the 13th century. The chancel which is a 'weeping chancel' and tower dates from the 14th century and the substantial tower had a base for a beacon fire. The nave was rebuilt in 1858 and the chancel refurbished and re-roofed in 1901. In the porch is an incised stone known as the 'leper stone'.

On the village green is a monolith erected in 1846 by Revd E. K. Jones. The stone had previously lain nearby. Also on the green is the post of a wheel cross, which was used as a whipping post or pillory.

The Dolphin Inn stands on Mill Lane south-east of the church. There were two corn mills in the village. The Upper Mill has disappeared but the Lower Mill is still in place complete with mill pond. Situated on Mill Lane below the church Lower Mill was built in 1803 and has an internal waterwheel. On the land south-west of the church are the remains of a lime kiln.

Lluest *Lodge*

Shown on the map as Pont-y-rhyl, Lluest is a small village in the Garw Valley between Llangeinor and Pontycymer on the east side of the river. Pont-y-rhyl is on the west bank and there is no direct road connection between the two. The village grew up to provide homes for the miners at Lluest Colliery, situated in the valley. The colliery was in operation prior to 1877 and there was an explosion in 1899, killing 19 men and boys. The pit which had employed 154 men in 1896 closed in 1902.

Nazareth Presbyterian Chapel above Bryn Villas on the east side of the valley was built in 1887 but is no longer a place of worship. The village once had a primary school but this has been demolished.

Margam

Roscoe in *Wanderings and Excursions in South Wales*, 1844, gives the following description: "Nothing can exceed the rural beauty of the modest hamlet of Margam, with its peaceful sanctuary occupying, as it does, the green valley at the base of the majestic mountain steep of Mynydd Mawr, clothed with verdant oaks to its very summit, and breasting with unrivalled grandeur the wild waves that sweep along the Bristol Channel. To the left of the village, and at a very short distance from it, spread the grounds and gardens of Margam Park, sharing alike the seclusion of the valley, and the shelter of the same lofty range of waving woods."

Margam until the 19th century included what became the town of Port Talbot and its suburb of Taibach as well as the urbanized part of Margam with its vast steelworks.

The area was inhabited in the pre-Roman era with Iron Age hillforts or enclosures at Moel Ton Mawr, Ton Mawr, Caer Blaen y Cwm, Mynydd y Castell, Geulan Las, Danish Camp at Cwm Philip and Half Moon Camp, Bronze Age barrows at Twmpath Diwlith, Mynydd Margam and a cairn of unknown date at Ergyd Uchaf. On a cairn on Mynydd Margam once stood the Bodvoc Stone, an inscribed stone of the 6th or 7th century which read 'BODVOCI HIC IACIT FILIUS CATOTIGIRNI PROENPUS ETERNALI VEDOMAVI' – 'Bodvoc. Here he lies, son of Cattegern and great-grandson of Eternalis Vedomavus'. A replica now stands in place of the original which forms part of a collection of old stones and crosses in the Old School House in Margam Park. The collection of 30 stones and crosses includes a Roman milestone, used later, turned upside down as a memorial stone inscribed 'HIC IACIT CANTVSVS PATER PAVLINVS', 'Here lies Cantusus his father was Paulinus'. On the reverse is the Latin 'IMPC FLA MAX MINO INVIC TO AV GVS', meaning 'Emperor Caesar Flavius Valerius Maximinus, the Unconquered, Augustus'. Among the Celtic crosses are the Cross of Einion and the magnificent Cross of Conbelin, possibly the finest in Wales.

According to Lewis, the original name of Margam "was Pen-dâr or Oak Summit, after the noble wood of oak that covers the breast of a mountain, upwards of eight hundred feet in height, forming a striking feature in the landscape." The name Margam is thought to be a

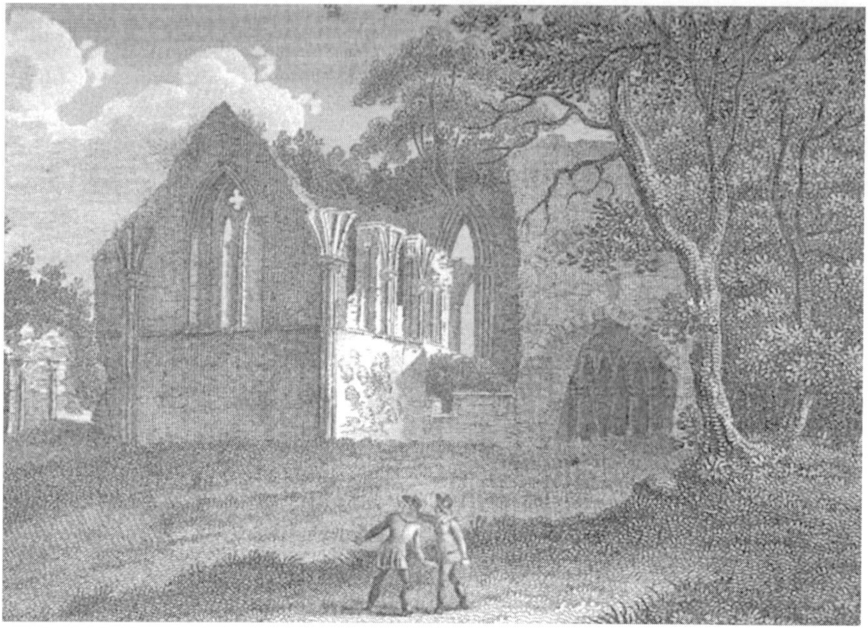

Margam Abbey

corruption of Mawrgan, who was the son of Caradoc ab Iestyn, lord of Afon and a great benefactor of the abbey.

Margam Abbey was founded by Robert Earl of Gloucester in 1147 who was buried there. Mawrgan and his sons continued to donate generously to the abbey which was a Cistercian house dedicated to St Mary. The Abbey took 40 years to build and was at the time the largest and wealthiest Cistercian foundation in Wales. There had been an earlier Welsh Bishopric on the site which later became part of Llandaff. It had also been the site of a residence of the Princes of Glamorgan.

The Abbey was known for its hospitality and among its guests was King John, who when exacting a levy from the Cistercian monasteries, exempted Margam, on account of the hospitality he had received there. Margam had the privilege of Sanctuary, a privilege restricted to about 30 abbeys and cathedrals in England and Wales following the Norman Conquest.

Geraldus Cambrensis in the 12th century tells the following story: "About the time of its foundation, a young man of those parts, by birth a Welshman, having claimed and endeavoured to apply to his own use certain lands which had been given to the monastery, by the instigation of the devil set on fire the best barn belonging to the monks, which was filled with corn; but, immediately becoming mad, he ran about the country in a distracted state, nor ceased raving until he was seized by his parents and bound. Having burst his bonds, and tired out his keepers, he came the next morning to the gate of the monastery, incessantly howling out that he was inwardly burnt by the influence of the monks, and thus in a few days expired, uttering the most miserable complaints."

He also relates how "a ship was sent to Bristol to purchase corn for charitable purposes. The vessel, delayed by contrary winds, and not returning (but rather affording an opportunity for the miracle), on the very day when there would have been a total deficiency of corn, both for the poor and the convent, a field near the monastery was found suddenly to ripen, more than a month before the usual time of harvest: thus, divine Providence supplied the brotherhood and the numerous poor with sufficient nourishment until autumn. By these and other signs of virtues, the place accepted by God began to be generally esteemed and venerated."

Part of the Abbey church remains as are the walls of the dodecahedral Early English chapter house. In *The Beauties of England and Wales* by Thomas Rees, in 1815 the church is described: "It is a fine specimen of pure Norman architecture. The circular arches of the nave, which rest on pilasters, are lofty; the windows are small, the tops formed of circular arches, and the western front is considerably ornamental. This building, through neglect, was rapidly falling into decay, but fortunately escaped the fate of the Chapter-house. The late Mr. Talbot caused it to be completely repaired, under the direction of competent persons, so that it now presents one of the most interesting objects of this class in the principality."

At the Dissolution, the Abbey and its possessions, together with the Royalty of Avon Water was purchased by Sir Rice Mansel of Penrice and Oxwich who built a mansion on the site. The family remained in possession until 1750 when the estate passed to Revd Thomas Talbot, the grandson of Thomas Mansel, 1st Baron Mansel. The present Margam Castle was built in the 1830s for Christopher Rice Mansel

Talbot in a Tudor Gothic style with an octagonal tower attached to which was a turreted staircase. The Castle was damaged by fire in 1977 but has been partially restored. C.R.M. Talbot represented Glamorgan in Parliament as a Liberal from 1830 until his death in 1890. He was a major shareholder in the South Wales Railway and saw the establishment of a major ironworks on his land in 1830, work carried on by his granddaughter Emily Charlotte Talbot.

In the grounds is the Orangery. Roscoe offers the following: "This place boasts one of the finest greenhouses in the kingdom, which contains the splendid collection of orange and lemon trees brought from Italy, by Sir Henry Wootton, as a present to King Charles I. The vessel in which it was freighted was wrecked on this estate nearly two centuries ago, and the plants were preserved to be restored to the Royal owner; but the troubles of that period prevented this from being done and they were afterwards confirmed to the present possessor

Margam Castle

by Queen Anne. At either end of the building are two superb saloons in which are placed several rare specimens of antiquity, some splendid vases, and precious subjects of sculpture." The Orangery built in 1787 of Pyle sandstone is 327 feet in length with a Palladian front of 27 windows. It still houses some orange trees but its principal role today is as a concert room, wedding and function venue.

The estate remained in the ownership of the Talbot family until 1942 when it was acquired by Sir David Edwards Bevan, owner of the Vale of Neath Brewery (see Cadoxton) and following his death in 1973 it was purchased by Glamorgan County Council.

Margam Park is now owned by Neath Port Talbot Council and is operated as a country park with various attractions and events. There is the deer park containing some 300 fallow deer, 64 red deer and 34 Pére David deer, a narrow gauge railway, lake, a citrus house as well as the Castle, Abbey ruin and church all set in 1,000 acres. The Park is open year round but opening times are restricted.

To the south of the Park is a small modern estate of houses built on what was a nunnery and the reservoir adjoining the M4 and the steelworks is called Eglwys Nunnydd or Nuns' Church Reservoir.

Mawdlam

Mawdlam is a small village immediately west of the M4 and the villages of Pyle and Kenfig Hill. Its name derives from the church of St Mary Magdalene which dates from the 13th century and was originally a chapel of ease to the church of St James at Kenfig. The church was renovated and enlarged in 1894, funded by Miss Emily Talbot of the nearby Margam Castle. Built on high ground, probably as a safeguard against the encroachment of the dunes, the squat tower is a landmark in the area. It is thought that the site of the church may have been a Celtic *llan*, given the almost circular form of the churchyard. The tower clock was installed in 1955 as a War Memorial. The font is Norman.

Adjacent to the church is the Angel Inn, thought to have originally been a *maledaria* or medieval hospital. (In medieval times the word hospital referred to a place of hospitality for pilgrims.) The building which in the 1940s was thatched underwent major structural changes in 1953.

The village consists of modern individual housing on a no through road, Heol Las. There is a place of worship attached to one of the houses.

Mayals

Mayals is a modern suburban community to the south of Swansea, adjacent to Mumbles. It contains the Clyne Valley Country Park, Clyne Castle, Clyne Gardens and the Clyne Golf Club.

The first records of Mayals are from the 14th century when John Yweyn, who held land at 'Maieles' was granted the right, in 1315, to divert 'all water and water courses within the fee of Oystermouth' for his mill. The exact location of this grist mill is unknown.

Clyne Castle was built in 1791 for Richard Phillips in a Classical style but remodelled in 1820 in the fashionable Gothic. It was acquired in 1860 by the Vivian family and in 1954 Castle and grounds were purchased by Swansea Council and the grounds became a public park. The Castle was bought by the University for student accommodation but has since been developed into apartments with a small housing development.

Clyne Gardens contain many tropical and rare plants together with a Japanese bridge, Admirals Tower and a Gazebo. There is also a small lake and the 1907 estate chapel designed by W. G. Vivian. The gardens are open year round and admission is free.

Clyne Valley Woods was the site of the Clyne Woods Arsenic and Copper works, built from 1825 and operated intermittently until 1860. The Ivy Tower in the Woods is the base of the old chimney stack to which a staircase, window, door and battlements have been added. The remnants of the works, which were situated to the east of the Ivy Tower, can still be seen in the form of pipes, flues and furnaces.

Further up the valley there were coal workings and the Clyne Colliery was operational in 1877 but had closed by 1900. The winding engine still remains in the woods as are the signs of bell pits, used to obtain coal from seams near the surface.

Merthyr Mawr *Great Martyr*

Merthyr Mawr is a gem of a village, with thatched cottages, a sheep dipping bridge, castle, church, swing bridge, ruined chapel and massive sand dunes.

The village is entered from the west over the 15th century New Inn Bridge though the inn was later. The holes in the walls of the bridge were for sheep that were herded onto the bridge and forced to jump into the deep waters of the River Ogmore below. There was once an inn near the bridge and its landlord at the time of the French Revolution was known as Cap Goch or Red Cap because of his headgear which imitated the French revolutionaries. The inn was a popular stopping place and attracted many traders carrying goods or money. Cap Goch would wine and dine his guests but a large number would disappear. Bodies were found washed up at the river mouth at Ogmore by Sea and suspicion fell on the inn. The disappearances continued but no further bodies were found until the inn was demolished some 80 years later. A cave was found under the inn full of robbed goods and in the garden the remains of his victims were discovered. What became of Cap Goch is uncertain. His true name is unknown but one theory is that he was hanged at Stalling Down for sheep stealing.

The village is entered over another bridge over the Ogmore, the New Bridge. The road passes through the parkland of Merthyr Mawr House,

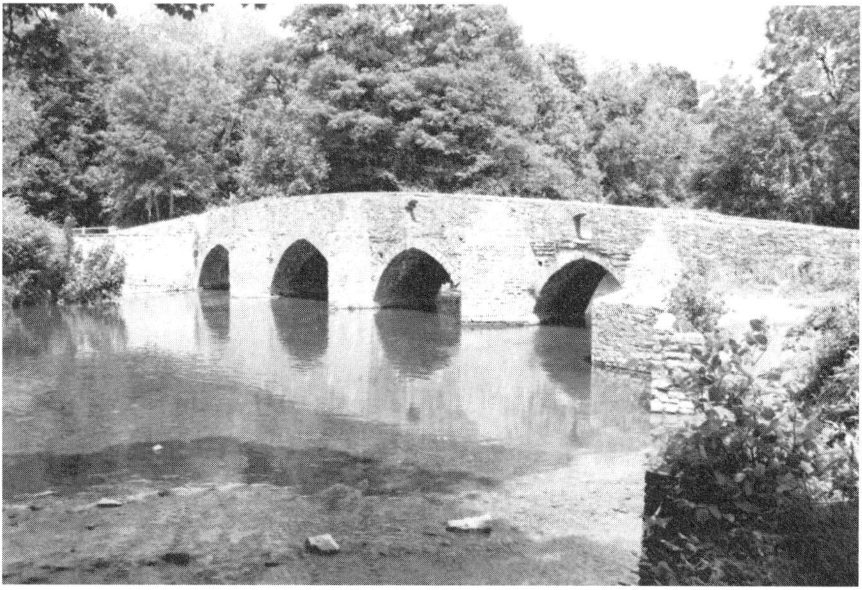

New Inn Bridge

built at the beginning of the 19th century by Sir John Nicholl, a leading lawyer, judge and Member of Parliament. Born in Llanmaes he spent most of his time in London and represented English constituencies, but owned estates in Glamorgan. He purchased the Merthyr Mawr estate, demolishing the previous house built by the Stradlings in the 16th century, in 1806. While his new home was being built he resided at Candleston Castle, which he eventually purchased in 1830. He moved into Merthyr Mawr House in 1809.

In woodland to the north of the house are the walls of the 15th century St Roque's Chapel. The chapel stands in what is thought to be an Iron Age defended enclosure.

The estate lodge is the first of a number of thatched cottages in the village.

A road leads down to the 1840 foot swing or suspension bridge, funded by Sir John Nicholl, which connects with a path to the stepping stones across the River Ewenny at Ogmore Castle. One local story is that the bridge replaced stepping stones which are now those in the River Ewenny. The road to the bridge crosses the leat that supplied Merthyr Mawr sawmill. The mill was used to cut the Sutton stone quarried from St Brides Major. The stone is said to be unique in that it can be sawn but subsequently hardens with weathering.

The Church of St Teilo was designed by Pugin's pupil Benjamin Ferrey, and built in 1848, replacing an earlier church on the site. It consists of a nave, chancel, south porch with a double bellcote and a small vestry to the north of the chancel. Of interest are some early medieval inscribed stones and a cross in a covered area behind the church. There are records of a monastic settlement in the village as far back as 862.

Beyond the village are the remains of Candleston Castle, a fortified manor house that was habitable into the 19th century. Candleston was built by the Norman Cantelupe family in the early 14th century. It was eventually abandoned because of the influx of sand from the Merthyr Mawr Warren, a great dune that extends to the mouth of the River Ogmore and across to Porthcawl. The dunes are the second highest in Europe and at one time stretched as far as Swansea to form the largest dune in Europe. It is now a National Nature Reserve and has SSSI status because of the plants that thrive there.

In 1765 William Bonvil died while net fishing in the sea at Merthyr Mawr. The inquest was informed that when he, with his two companions drew "the said net ashore having therein only one little flat fish called a sole, about five inches in length, did (as usual by fishermen), in order to take the said fish out of the net, being there entangled, take hold thereof by the head with his teeth; and afterwards inadvertently loosening his holt, the said fish slipt forwards into his mouth and throat so far that the same could only be felt by the tail; by which position of the said fish the breath of the said William Bonvil was stopt, and thereupon he languished for about twenty minutes and then and there died."

Cliffe records an unusual method of fishing in the River Ogmore at Merthyr Mawr. "When the river is low and the tide is on the ebb, the fishermen station themselves with their cur dogs at the mouth, and 'club' the sewin and salmon as they endeavour to escape across the shallows to the sea. The dogs are trained to seize the fugitives, and the struggles of men and animals constitute an animated and entertaining scene; the dogs often leave an ugly mark in the back of the fish."

Middleton

Middleton is a hamlet east of Rhossili on the B4247. Ship Farm was once the Ship Inn and dates from 1763. To the north is the Rhossili Activity Centre, housed in the former school and only available to groups.

Mumbles and Oystermouth

The original village was Oystermouth and The Mumbles referred to Mumbles Head and the two rocks standing at the end of Swansea Bay. Today the two communities are often referred to as Mumbles.

According to Morgan in *The Place Names of Wales*, "The name was given originally to designate the detached rocks at the end of the headland, but in course of time it was extended to the old village of Oystermouth. Col. Francis derives the name from mammals, which word gives a very fair description of the two rounded breast-like rocks in the place."

It is thought that Oystermouth is a corruption of Ystum Llwynarth which itself is thought to be a corruption of Ystum Lluarth Garth meaning shape of the buttressed entrenchment, referring to Oystermouth Castle.

Mumbles lies four miles south-west of Swansea and was until 1960 connected by a sea front railway. Originally called the Oystermouth Railway it was built in 1804 to carry coal, iron ore and limestone to the docks at Swansea. In 1807 however it became the first fare paying passenger railway service in the world, with horse drawn carriages. After initial success, the opening of a turnpike road saw the decline of the railway which was revived in 1855 and had a steam service from 1877, though a horse service continued until 1896. In 1898 the line was extended to Mumbles Head. In 1929 electric trams were introduced. These double deck vehicles had a capacity of 106

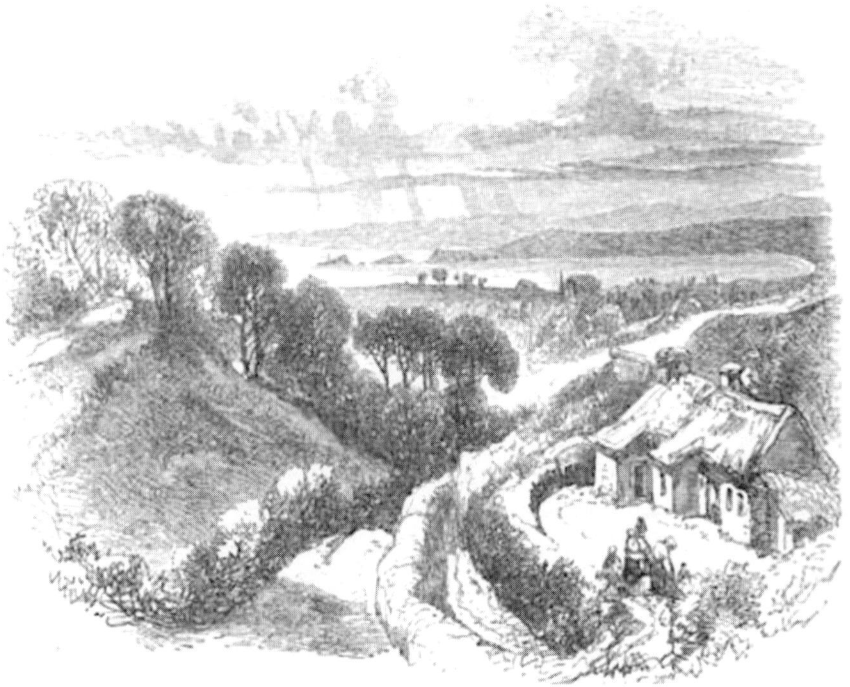

Old view of Swansea Bay and Mumbles Head

passengers and were often operated in pairs. In 1959 the railway was acquired by the local bus company, South Wales Transport and closed.

Samuel Lewis comments: "The village is much resorted to by visitors during the summer; but, from its peculiar situation under a high limestone rock, which deprives it of the sun for several months in the winter, is a very dreary residence during that season. The surrounding scenery, though rather bold and striking, has little either of a picturesque or pleasing character; but the high grounds command noble views over the bays of Swansea and Carmarthen, the peninsula of Gower, which separates them, and the Bristol Channel. The oyster fishery is carried on during the season to a considerable extent, chiefly for the supply of the Bristol market; and salmon are frequently procured from the weirs on the shores of Swansea bay. The Mumbles Point, an insulated rock at high water, forms the western extremity of Swansea bay; and the trustees of the harbour have erected a lighthouse upon it, which has been productive of the greatest benefit to vessels navigating this coast, and is supported by a small toll payable by each vessel passing within a certain distance of it. The Mumbles Roads provide excellent shelter, with good anchorage, for ships navigating the channel, which frequently put in here during the prevalence of westerly gales, to the number, occasionally, of two hundred sail."

All Saints Church dates from 1147 but the small Norman church is dwarfed by Penson's 1860 and Barnard's 1916 enlargements. The old church has been relegated to form the south aisle and Lady Chapel, but retains an ancient pillar *piscina* and an early medieval font.

There is a stained glass window depicting the Mumbles Railway, one commemorating the 1883 lifeboat disaster when four men died and another commemorating the 1947 Mumbles Lifeboat disaster when eight men died trying to rescue the crew of the SS Santamper off Sker Point.

In the graveyard is the tomb of Thomas Bowdler who lived at a house called Rhyddings in what is now the Brynmill area, at the time of his death in 1825. Bowdler, a physician, published the first volume of *The Family Shakspeare* in 1807. It was intended for women and children and omitted or changed certain words Bowdler deemed obscene, so Lady Macbeth's 'Out Damned Spot' became 'Out crimson spot'. Later editions used the more commonly accepted spelling 'Shakespeare'. He also published an expurgated version of Gibbons'

Decline and Fall of the Roman Empire. His name is now used in the term 'bowdlerize', meaning expurgate. In his will, Bowdler made gifts to the poor of Swansea and his extensive library was donated to the newly created University College of St David in Lampeter.

Three bells in All Saints Church once belonged to the fire damaged Jesuit church of La Campana in Santiago, Chile. They were returned to Chile in 2011.

Baring-Gould asserts that Oystermouth Castle "is one of the finest in Wales. "Sir," said Dr. Johnson, "you may pack all the Scottish castles into one in Wales"."

The date of the establishment of Oystermouth Castle is open to conjecture, but the first earthworks were probably built by William de Londres (1107-1131) and destroyed by the Welsh in 1136. It is thought that the keep was built by Maurice de Londres who succeeded his father. The castle was destroyed by the Welsh in 1215,

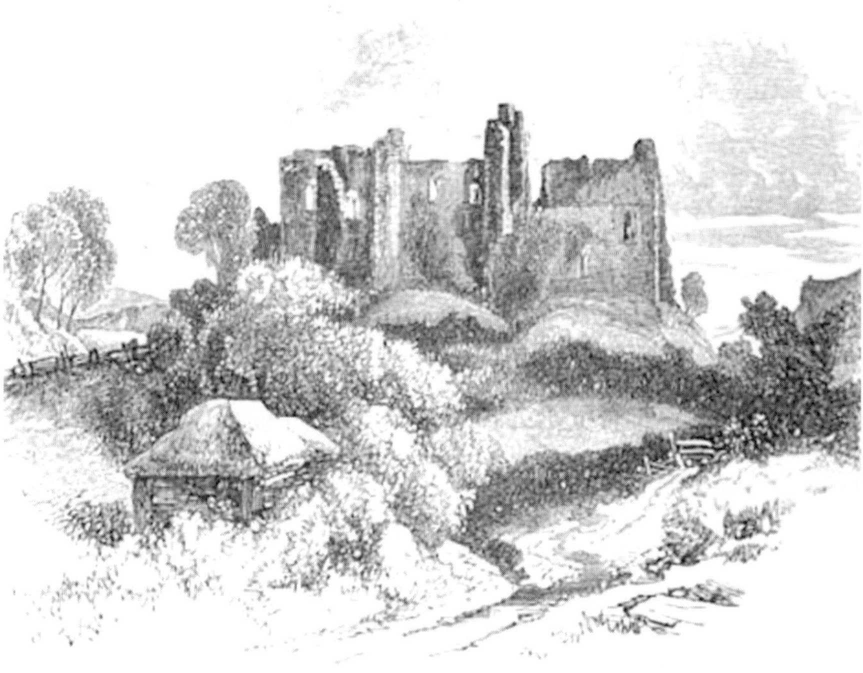

Oystermouth Castle

the first written record of the castle, and again in 1217. By this time the de Londres line had died out and Oystermouth was in the hands of the Lord of Gower. The de Braose family undertook the rebuilding of the castle and in 1284 William de Braose entertained Edward I there on the 10th and 11th December, though his principal castle was Swansea. Oystermouth was again taken by the Welsh in 1287 and in the 1400 rebellion of Owain Glyndwr. By 1432 the castle was in a poor condition.

The castle is still the most impressive in the area and is the setting for concerts. The chapel window of the 14th century is a particular feature and following work in 2011 the chapel is accessed by a glass bridge. It is open daily, 11.00 to 17.00 during the spring and summer.

The castle is said to be haunted by a 'lady in white', a crying ghost with a bloodstained back.

Mumbles retains its attractions for visitors, with Bracelet, Limeslade and Langland Bays to the south and its promenade. Mumbles pier was opened in 1898 and served as the terminus for the Mumbles Railway and was also served by steamers crossing to Lundy Island, Ilfracombe and Weston Super Mare. A life boat station was built in the 1920s with a walkway from the pier. The pier and a new lifeboat station are due to reopen in 2014 after extensive renovation. The art deco Tivoli cinema is now an amusement arcade.

Mumbles has a good selection of shops, cafés, restaurants and pubs, though the number of bars has fallen dramatically from twenty to five. The Mumbles Mile was notorious for parties attempting to drink in every bar and pressure from the local community coupled with the growth in clubs and bars in Swansea caused the decline. In 1839 the recommended hotel was the Old Mermaid which later became the Beaufort Arms, though this closed in the 1920s. The building is situated next to The George.

The Mumbles Lighthouse which stands on the outer of the two islands was designed by William Jernegan and constructed between 1791 and 1795. The light was originally two coal-fires, but converted to oil-burning in 1798-99. The cast-iron and glass lantern was built at the Neath Abbey Ironworks. It was replaced in 1977.

A fort was built on the outer island as a defence against the French in 1860 and continued in service until decommissioning in the 1950s.

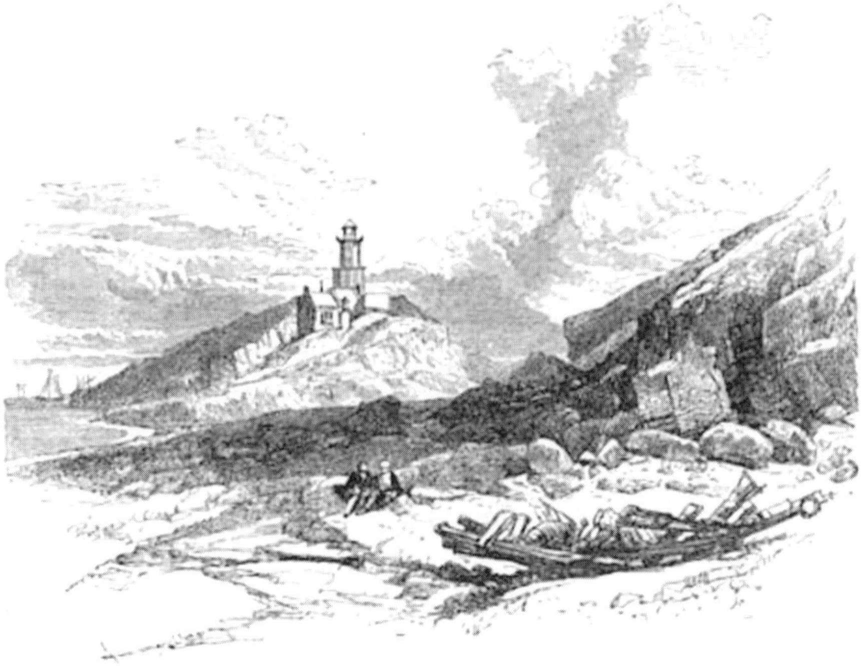

The Mumbles Lighthouse

On the corner of Mumbles Road and Myrtle Terrace is the Prince's Fountain, built in 1863 to celebrate the wedding of Prince Edward and Princess Alexandra.

On Mumbles Hill there are the remains of Second World War anti aircraft batteries. A circular battery was replaced by two square batteries in 1944. The Hill was also the site of a flagstaff used by the Admiralty.

There are a number of chapels, all of which are still in use. Castleton Independent Chapel in Newton Road was built in 1902. The large and impressive Dunns Lane Methodist Chapel, on the corner of Mumbles Road and Dunns Lane, was built in 1877. Tabernacle Independent Chapel, now the United Reformed Church on the corner of Newton Road and Chapel Street was built in 1831 and rebuilt in 1870. Mount Zion Hall, Christadelphian Ecclesia was built in 1850.

Our Lady of the Sea Roman Catholic Church was built in 1909-1916 on the Promenade Terrace.

Murton

The old hamlet of Murton which lies north-east of Bishopston in Gower, has expanded dramatically in recent years with developments of houses and bungalows to the south but the area around Murton Green retains its character with its chapel village shops and the Plough and Harrow pub. To the north is the Green with its cricket pitch, Murton Sports and Social Club and open heathland.

Murton Wesleyan Methodist Church was established in 1828 and rebuilt in 1897.

South of the village, east of the southern end of Long Acre is the site of St Peter's Well, Chapel and priest's house. The single cell chapel was thought to date from the 6th century. The area was excavated in 1895 when there were two intact walls and a window and the well had three side walls. Today the well is just a small depression and the chapel remains have succumbed to the ravages of time and nature.

Nantyfyllon

The name according to legend is derived from Nant-y-ffyrling, meaning Farthing stream after the story that a farthing coin thrown into the stream changed into a gold sovereign.

Nantyffyllon is a former mining village half a mile north of Maesteg. Mining came in the 1820s to the Llynfi valley and by 1877 the mountainsides to the east and west were littered with old mine workings and quarries. The Dyffryn Pit occupied the area where the industrial park is now situated. It had closed by 1899. The real expansion of the village came after the sinking of the Coegnant Colliery in 1883. Built to the north-east of the village, Coegnant was started by the Llynfi Coal and Iron Company but was taken over by North Navigation Collieries in 1889. At its height, Coegnant employed over 2,000 men and it continued in production until 1981.

The village has a few shops, a post office and a school and there has been some new housing, mainly along Heol Ty Gwyn and Dyffryn Madog. There are two pubs remaining, the Elderbush and the Masons Arms Inn.

Nantyffyllon Workmen's Hall was opened in 1926 with a public hall seating 680, a smaller hall, library and reading room. Plans for recreational facilities were abandoned in the light of the poor economy at the time.

St Peter's Church was built in 1886-7 on a new site given to the Ecclesiastical Commissioners jointly by I. G. R. Homfray of Penllyn Castle and Revd Robert C. Lvnche-Blosse vicar of Coaley in Gloucestershire. It is now a private dwelling. It will be noted that there are Blosse and Homfray Streets in the village named after the church's benefactors.

Salem Welsh Baptist chapel, Picton Street was built in 1852, rebuilt in 1872 and 1908, but no longer in use. Saron Welsh Independent chapel in Dyffryn Row was built in 1853, rebuilt in 1900 and is still in use. Siloh Independent chapel in High Street was built in 1841, modified or rebuilt in 1858, 1876 and 1911, but is no longer in use. Jerusalem Calvinistic Methodist Chapel in Picton Street was built in 1901 and modified, in 1904. It was taken over by the Jehovah's Witnesses as their Kingdom Hall. Trinity Calvinistic Methodist Chapel in Bangor Street was built in 1895 and is still in use.

Nantymoel *The Bare Stream*

Nantymoel is a former mining village at the top of the Ogmore Valley. The road to the north climbs to the Bwlch Mountain and across to the Rhondda Valley or to the Llynfi and Afan valleys. There had been small scale coal mining in the valley for some years, but in August 1865 the Ogmore Valley railway opened with its terminus at Nantymoel and mining took off. In 1873 the Western Merthyr Coal and Fuel Company started the Edwards Colliery, also known as the Blaenogwr and later the Western Ocean or Ocean Colliery. It was taken over by the Ocean Coal Company Ltd who operated it until nationalization in 1947. The colliery employed nearly 1,000 men and in 1957 it linked underground with the Wyndham Colliery. The combined colliery closed in 1984.

By 1879 there were a series of rows of terraced housing, including Chapel Row (later Chapel Street) and Tenby Row together with a hotel, station and two chapels. By 1900 the village had developed to what is recognizable today, with an electric light works to the rear of Court Colman Street.

Chapels proliferated. Saron Welsh Baptist chapel on Station Road was first built in 1874, rebuilt in 1877 and modified in 1901. It fell into disuse in the 1990s and its site is now occupied by a pair of semi detached houses. Bethel Independent Chapel in Commercial Street was built in 1867 and rebuilt in 1872. Mount Zion Independent Chapel on Station Road was built in 1882. Dinam Calvinistic Methodist Chapel was built in 1874 on the corner of Dinam Street and Dinam Close. It has now been demolished. Gilead English Calvinistic Methodist Chapel was built on Dinam Street in 1878 but demolished by 1998. Horeb Baptist Chapel was built facing Chapel Street in 1894.

Plans for the Welsh church of St Peter in Station Road Nantymoel were drawn by E. M. B. Vaughan in 1887-90, and the church opened in 1890. St Paul's English Church was opened in 1909 above Commercial Street. St Peter's closed and was demolished in 1960 and St Paul's Church's dedication was changed to St Peter and St Paul. That church closed in 1992 and was converted into a private dwelling with an unusual observatory built alongside the bellcote. The subsequent owner also changed the name to St David's.

Nantymoel was a busy village with an array of shops, many of which are now closed. The old colliery site has been landscaped, but there are traces across the mountainsides of tram roads, aerial ropeways, trial mines, air shafts and quarries. The village school remains.

Neath Abbey

The village of Neath Abbey lies across the river from the town of Neath. It has a large industrial area with its roots in the 17th century when an iron works was established. It is a village well worth a visit for its religious and industrial heritage.

The village has a large modern housing development occupying a former grange of Neath Abbey and the Cwrt Herbert Playing Fields with the Neath Sports Centre. There is a Tesco superstore and on the road beyond it leading to Skewen are two pubs, the Smiths Arms and the Hope and Anchor. Also on New Road are the ruins of the northern gatehouse and porter's lodge of Neath Abbey.

Neath Abbey was founded by Richard de Granville, brother of Robert Fitzhamon, Lord of Glamorgan, with a gift of land to the convent of Savigny near Lyons by a charter which stipulated that a monastery of

Grey Friars should be established at Neath. The Abbey itself was founded in 1130 and by 1147 the Savigniac Order had been absorbed into the Cistercian Order. The first Abbot was Bichard who died in 1145. The Abbey was rebuilt in the late 13th century, the earlier building becoming too small for the growing community. The Abbey was further enriched by a gift by Roger Earl of Warwick of land and fisheries in Gower.

Edward II, following his escape from Bristol, found refuge for a short time at Neath Abbey in 1326 before his capture and murder at Berkeley Castle in Gloucestershire in 1327. At the time of the Dissolution there were just eight monks at the Abbey and the last abbot was John Lleision. The estate was granted to Sir Richard Williams by Henry VIII. Rowlands in his *Historical Notes*, 1866, described the abbey with the words: "The present ruins give a very inadequate idea of its magnificence. The dusky smoke of the neighbouring works has destroyed its picturesque appearance and its beauty."

Cliffe in *The Book of South Wales, the Bristol Channel, Monmouthshire, and the Wye* of 1848 offers the following observation: "Little did Richard and Constance de Granville, the first benefactors of the Abbey of Neath, when in the year 1129 they witnessed the solemn

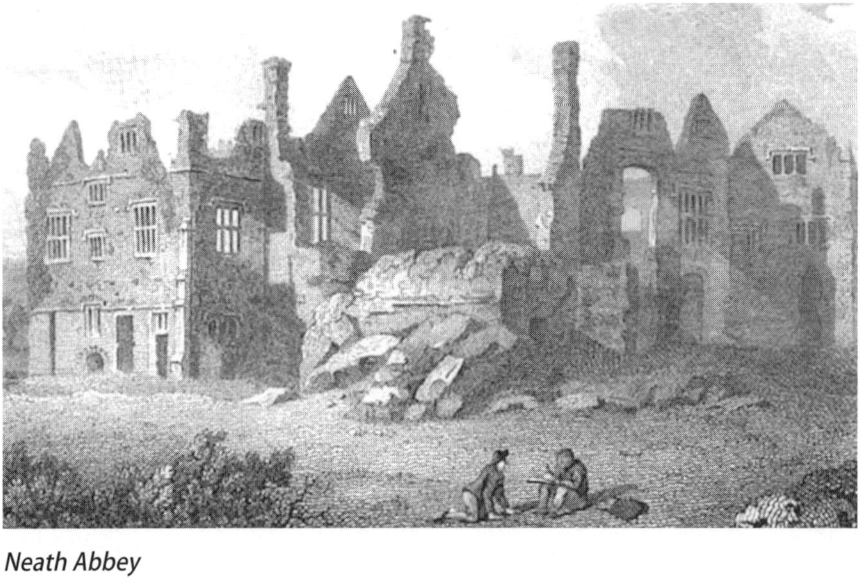

Neath Abbey

dedication of the sacred structure to the Holy Trinity – little did the community of Grey Friars, from Savigny, near Lyons, who had taken up their abode in this fair spot at the earnest wish of the Norman Lord and Lady – imagine that it would be desecrated by the worship of Mammon, become a smoky ruin, scarcely distinguishable by the passing traveller from the forges, the furnaces, the chimneys, or the squalid outworks of manufacturing establishments by which it is surrounded! The Anthem of Praise and Thanksgiving has been superseded by the clank of the steam-engine and the roar of fires. Strange mutation! Yet the old Abbey is pleasant to look upon. It is a memento amidst the turmoil of life. It speaks eloquently of a Future. It is full of interest to the lover of antiquity."

Leland in the 16th century described "Neth, an Abbey of White Monks, a mile above Neth town, standing also in the ripe [bank] of Neth. It seemed to me the fairest Abbey in all Wales."

The Welsh Bard Lewis Morgannwg in 1520 gave the following description:

"Like the sky of the Vale of Ebron is the covering of this monastery: weighty is the lead that roofs this abode – the dark blue canopy of the dwellings of the godly. Every colour is seen in the crystal windows, every fair and high-wrought form beams forth through them like the rays of the nun – Portals of radiant guardians!

Pure and empyrial, here is every dignified language, and every well skilled preceptor. Here are seen the graceful robes of prelates, here may he found gold and jewels, the tribute of the wealthy.

Here also is the gold-adorned choir, the nave the gilded tabernacle-work, the pinnacles, worthy of the Three Fountains. Distinctly may be seen on the glass, imperial arms; a ceiling resplendent with Kingly bearings, and on the surrounding border the shields of princes! the arms of Neath, of a hundred ages; there is the white freestone and the arms of the best men under the crown of Harry; and the church walls of grey marble. The vast and lofty roof is like the sparkling heavens on high, above are seen archangels' forms; the floor beneath is for the people of earth, all the tribe of Babel, for them it is wrought of variegated stone. The bells, the benedictions, and the peaceful songs of praise, proclaim the frequent thanksgiving of the white monks."

Neath Abbey came under the care of the state in 1944 and gradually

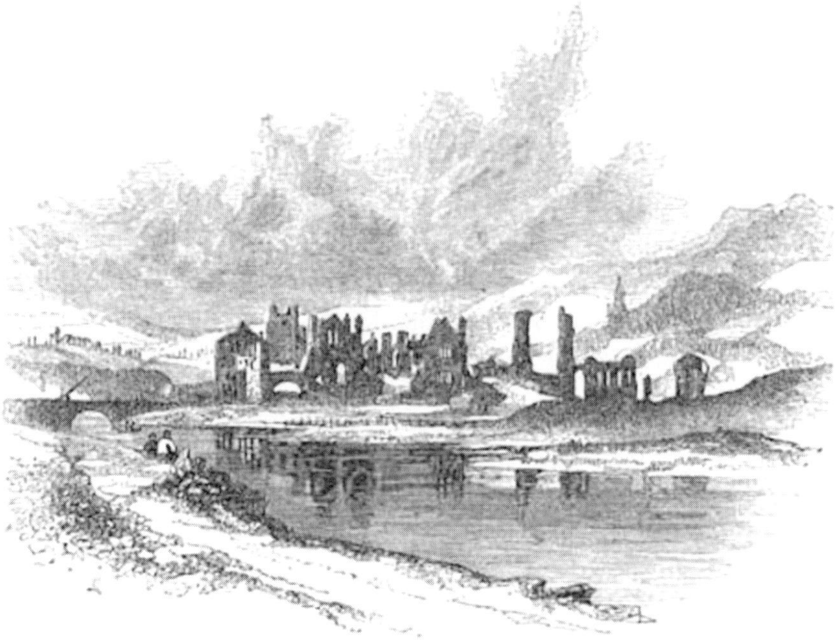

Neath Abbey

the signs of industrial use, the abbey precinct was used as a copper smelting and casting workshop, have been removed. After the Dissolution the south-eastern part of the cloister ranges was converted into a grand mansion which was occupied throughout the 17th century by the Herbert family. There are extensive ruins of the Abbey church, mansion, west range which was home to the lay brothers and the monks' dormitory and undercroft. In the care of Cadw the abbey is open daily from 10.00 a.m. to 4.00 p.m.

The first heavy industry commenced prior to 1694 in the form of a copper works built to the west of the Abbey by the Mines Royal Company. The site was later used for rolling iron plates and later still as a woollen mill.

Neath Abbey Ironworks was established in the 18th century and the impressive remains of its two blast furnaces are on Longford Road. Associated with the iron works was an engine works producing its first railway engine, the *Speedwell*, in the late 1820s. The works closed in 1885.

The Cheadle Copperworks were established in 1760 some 300 yards south-west of the abbey on a site now buried under the A465 dual carriageway. The furnaces were removed in 1821. The site was taken over and became the Cheadle shipbuilding yard complete with dry dock, the shipbuilding arm of the Neath Abbey Ironworks.

The main industrial area today is adjoining the A465 and is light industrial or commercial.

Situated in Taillwyd Road is Moriah Independent Chapel built in 1906.

Newton (Porthcawl)

Situated on the outskirts of Porthcawl, Newton is an ancient village, the Church of St John the Baptist dating from the 12th century. However even earlier is the site of a Neolithic house to the north of the village on Newton Down. Excavating a Bronze Age round barrow in 1952, it was discovered that it had been built over a Neolithic hut evidenced by a sandstone floor and shards of Neolithic pottery. There are also the remains of a 3rd or 4th century Roman Villa just to the north of Orchard Drive. Lewis, in 1848, traced the Julia Strata Maritima Roman road on Newton Down.

Leigh's *Guide to Wales* in 1839 describes Newton as a small village, which has risen to the rank of a watering-place since the beginning of the present century. The beach is well sheltered by limestone cliffs, and bathing-machines are kept here. The sands, however, drift considerably, and are not well adapted for promenading.

The village has expanded considerably in the last century, becoming a retirement and commuting centre but at the heart of the village remain the church, village green and the Jolly Sailor and Ancient Briton pubs. There is a post office, service station, mini supermarket, and other small shops as well as the Globe Inn away from the green. The village has two independent day schools, St John's for boys and St Clare's which is co-educational and attached to St Clare's Convent in the village.

The first mention of the church is in 1189, but it was largely rebuilt in the late 15th or early 16th century. The four storey tower is topped with a saddleback roof and inside the projecting stone pulpit is particularly striking with a rudely carved representation of the scourging of Christ. There are also the remnants of wall paintings and squints. In the churchyard is a preaching cross. The base is original but the shaft and cross date from 1890.

South of the church is St John's Well or Sandford Well, a stone structure with slab stairs descending. The water was reputed to have miraculous or healing qualities and according to Camden ebbed and flowed in opposition to the tide, being full at low water and empty at high water. Lewis comments that "various conjectures have been formed to account for this phenomenon, which may be satisfactorily explained on the principle of a natural syphon".

Hope Free Congregational Chapel was built in 1827 and rebuilt in 1887.

The major part of the village is modern but there are some attractive older cottages and houses.

There is a sandy beach which stretches from Newton Point to the estuary of the River Ogmore, though there is an outcrop of rocks known as Black Rocks. The land to the east of the village forms part of the Merthyr Mawr Warren, though much of the sand is now covered

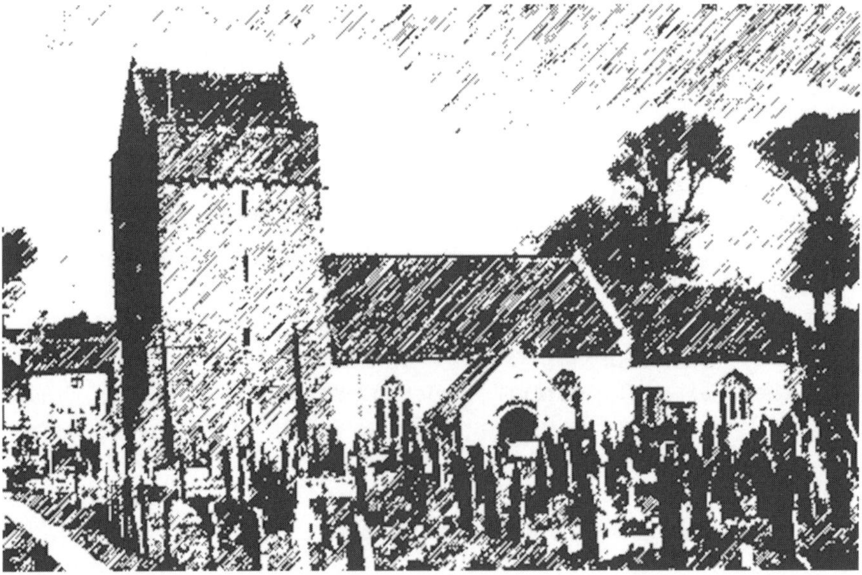

Newton Church

in greenery. Just north of the warren is the Wig Fach Caravan Park while to the south-west of the village is the massive Trecco Bay caravan park. Rees noted “The shore is very commodious for bathing; and there is a house here for the reception of company, which belongs to the landlord of the Pyle Inn, there being no inn in the place”.

The residents of the village were not always as honest as they should have been. Lewis reports “No public charities now exist, in consequence of a bequest of £50 by Mary Lougher, in 1731, and a similar one of £10 by Alexander Pryce or Rees, prior to 1786, having been misapplied, and partly to his own use, by one of the parish officers”.

Newton (Swansea)

Newton in 1880 was a peaceful farming hamlet, with a small number of large gentry houses such as Newton Manor House, built in 1861 in the style of a French Chateau, with French builders used in its construction. Today Newton is described as an affluent commuter suburb, west of Mumbles with Langland Bay to the south.

The centre of the village retains its charm, while the remainder of the village, spread out from the centre, has a mix of housing largely from the mid 20th century to the ultra modern.

One of the early buildings was Paraclete Congregational Chapel, built in 1818, rebuilt in 1880. St Peter’s Church was built in 1903 by the architect E. M. B. Vaughan, to serve Newton , Langland and Caswell. It became a parish church in 1933. This large Gothic styled church has three aisles and while cruciform, the aisles and vestries tend to mask the transepts from outside.

The village has a number of shops including a butchers, a primary school and the Newton Inn and Rock and Fountain.

Langland Bay to the south of Newton once had four hotels. Only the old Wittenburg has survived in a reduced form as the Little Langland Hotel. The Scottish baronial residence of Llan y Llan was built by the Crawshays, the Merthyr Tydfil ironmasters as their summer retreat. It later became the Langland Bay Hotel, then a convalescent home and is now split into luxury apartments and named Langland Bay Manor. The beach front is lined with beach huts and there is a café. The beach is popular in summer as the closest of the Gower beaches to Swansea. The 18 hole Langland Golf Course lies to the west, built on the site of Langland Farm following its sale in 1906.

Nicholaston

Nicholaston is a scattered village north of Oxwich Bay. The church of St Nicholas is believed to have been re-sited alongside the A4118 after the original site was inundated by sand. This medieval church was rebuilt in 1894 at the expense of Miss Olive Talbot in memory of her father, C. R. M. Talbot of Margam and Penrice, and is in high Victorian style by the architect George Halliday. The bell is dated 1518 and the font is carved from a stalagmite. The church has a nave, chancel, western bellcote and a large north porch with a statue of St Nicholas above.

To the north of the A4118 are the remains of a large Neolithic chambered long cairn, measuring 120 feet by 67 feet, but largely destroyed by quarrying and excavation, standing just four feet high.

The houses in the village are away from the main road and to the south there are holiday camping and caravan sites.

Norton (Mumbles)

Norton is an attractive seaside suburban village immediately north of Oystermouth. There has been extensive development since 1970. The older part of the village was slightly inland on Westcross Avenue which has the Mission Church which also acts as the village hall. The Mission church was opened in 1908 in a tin hut. It was replaced in 1990 by the present building. Just along the road is the Beaufort pub. There was once a Temperance Hotel on Alexandra Terrace on the sea front where the Mumbles Railway had the Norton Road Station.

On the hill above the village was a Bronze Age barrow, excavated in 1969 ahead of the building of Highmead Avenue and Lambourne Drive.

Nottage *Welsh Notais*

Nottage is part of the parish of Newton Nottage. There is some confusion as to the derivation of the name with Thomas Morgan believing it to be a corruption of 'Nuttage' while others give it as 'pollard ash tree'. Situated a mile to the north of Porthcawl, it has in the last fifty years expanded to become a suburb of the town. The picturesque old village retains its distinct identity with its enclosed village green opposite the Rose and Crown inn, narrow lanes and chapels. The older pub in the village is the Farmers Arms which backs onto the green. In the 12th century, Noche Court was a grange attached to Margam Abbey, producing wheat. At the Dissolution Nottage was sold to Sir Rice Mansel and in 1545 to the Lougher family with the house then known as Ty Mawr being rebuilt around 1570 as an Elizabethan stone rendered three storey mansion, as it remains today. In 1855 the then owner, Revd Henry Hay Knight, renamed the house Nottage Court. The house remains in private ownership. In the grounds is a Roman milestone with an Ogham inscription, removed to the garden from Port Talbot docks.

The Llynfi and Porthcawl Railway passed through the village with a small tunnel under the roadway to the east of the green. The line of the railway can still be seen between Moor Lane and the farm on Pyle Road.

There is no church in the village, though it is thought that it was the site of a Celtic church. Heol y Capel denotes the site of a medieval chapel and graveyard, though the precise location is unclear. Nottage General Baptist and Unitarian Church was built during the late eighteenth century and rebuilt around 1840.

At the northern end of Moor Lane is St David's Well set in a stone slab, roofed stone enclosure in a small dell known since the 12th century as Dewiscumbe. Another well, Ffynnon Fawr is a restored medieval well which once supplied the village and, in its early days, the port of Porthcawl with water. It is situated at the traffic roundabout at the entrance to the village from Pyle. The stone forming the stile is thought to come from the old chapel.

The village has a primary school, village store, newsagent and hairdressers. The main development in the village which consists of houses and bungalows has a small central shopping area with the Seagull Inn around a landscaped green.

Ogmore Vale

Ogmore Vale is a former mining village in the Ogmore Valley. According to Llwyd the derivation of Ogmore was 'eog' meaning salmon and 'mor' meaning water and before the mining in the valley the river was known for its salmon, with tales of dogs being trained to catch the fish in the lower reaches. Prior to the railway's arrival in 1865, there was no village, but five collieries saw a rapid expansion in the population and Ogmore Vale became the commercial centre for the villages of Wyndham, Nantymoel, Pricetown and Lewistown. As well as shops, the village boasted a skating rink, public swimming baths and two cinemas.

Among the shops was the Gwalia Stores, which were dismantled and moved to St Fagan's Museum in 1988. The site is now occupied by sheltered accommodation.

The Aber Colliery at Tynewydd, close to the present fire station, was opened in 1865 and continued until 1914, employing over 170 men. Penllwyngwent Colliery opened in 1906, in what is now a car breakers yard. Employing over 700 men at one point, it continued in operation until 1969. The Rhondda Main Colliery operated between 1914 and 1924. Situated to the south of the village at what later became a coal washery it employed up to 1,000 men. Tynewydd Colliery situated to the west of the new primary school started in 1865 and continued in operation until 1906, employing 204 men at its peak in 1896. Caedu Colliery operated to the south of Tynewydd and had closed by 1899. There is, however, more evidence of this colliery remaining than others, with the ruins of mine buildings and a blacksmith shop as well as a winding wheel and tramways.

The village prospered with an array of shops. The Workmen's Hall and Institute, an impressive public hall, opened in 1911. It could seat 1,000 and had a billiard room, library and smaller meeting rooms. Damaged by flooding in 1981, it was demolished in 1983.

Ogmore Vale Wesleyan Methodist Chapel on Tynewydd Row was built in 1886 but has now been converted into a furniture and carpet showroom. Bethlehem Baptist Chapel was built in 1871 and rebuilt in 1876 and is now used as a hall for performances. Bethania Independent Chapel on Bethania Row was built in 1848 and rebuilt in 1876. It is no longer in use as a chapel. The Primitive Methodist Chapel in Corbett Street was built in 1877 but is no longer in use. Ogwr Congregational Chapel was built in 1872 and rebuilt in 1902 and is now known as Christchurch United Reformed Church. Bethel Methodist Chapel in the High Street was built in 1907 but no longer in use. Hermon Baptist Chapel was built in 1876. The site is now occupied by a block of flats. Philadelphia Baptist Chapel was built in 1895 and is now the Kingdom Hall of the Jehovah's Witnesses at the southern entrance to the village.

St John's Church was built at the north end of St John Street as a corrugated iron structure in 1900. It was replaced by a stone church in 1914 which was closed in 2004 and demolished. There was a Roman Catholic Church in River Street but this had been taken over as St John's church hall by 1975. There is now a children's play area on the site.

In recent years the village has seen some new housing and a new primary school opened in 2003. The school houses a memorial listing every miner killed in the Ogmore Valley between 1864 and 1984. There is a range of shops, the Corbett Arms and the Fox and Hounds as well as a number of clubs. There is a small industrial estate to the north of the village.

Oldwalls

Oldwalls is a hamlet half a mile west of Llanrhidian in Gower. There is the Greyhound Inn and holiday accommodation. Ebenezer Calvinistic Methodist Chapel was built in 1850 and rebuilt in 1932.

Onllwyn

Onllwyn is a former mining village in the upper Dulais valley. The name appears to be a transposition of Llwyn On, the ash grove.

The village is small but has a welfare hall. It relies for its shops on the nearby village of Dyffryn Cellwen.

Mining was carried on to the south and west of the village with the first drifts opened in the 1840s by Evans and Bevan, a company that continued to operate the collieries until nationalization in 1945. There were four drifts in total employing 1,200 men in 1945. The collieries had closed by 1964. A rail line was established in 1864 and continues in use today for coal shipments from the Onllwyn Distribution Centre. The railway was once part of the Neath and Brecon line, with a station at Onllwyn. It closed to passenger traffic in 1962. There was an ironworks with two blast furnaces situated between Wembley Avenue and the railway. It closed in 1878 and there are no visible remains.

Oxwich

Oxwich is a pretty little village retaining some of its chocolate box thatched cottages along the narrow lane to the Oxwich Bay Hotel and leading to the beautiful sweep of Oxwich Bay. The bay, protected from the south-west by Oxwich Point, has a two and a half mile stretch of sand and is one of the best beaches in Britain. The suffix 'wich' is derived from the Norse 'wic' meaning creek or bay.

Oxwich was once a port exporting limestone, with up to 300 ships a year.

Oxwich Castle was in the hands of the De la Mere family until the 13th century when it passed by marriage to the Penrice family and subsequently, also through marriage, to Philip Mauncell who was in possession in 1459. The family lost possession through their support of the Lancastrians in the Wars of the Roses, but the estates were restored to Jenkin Mansel by Henry VII.

In 1520 Oxwich was selected by Sir Rhys Mansel for the site of his new fortified manor house of Oxwich Castle which still stands to the west of the bay, built on the site of the former De la Mere castle. It was enlarged by Sir Edward Mansel before being abandoned as the family seat in favour of Margam Abbey. In its day it was a large luxurious residence with courtyard, inside toilets and a large hall, but the main part of the building fell into decay with just part used as a farmhouse. In 1949 Lady Apsley gifted the castle to the nation and its now in the hands of Cadw and open to the public during the summer.

The church of St Illtyd stands on the site of a 6th century cell at the western end of the beach surrounded by trees. The present church dates from the 13th century with a 14th century east window and tower. Inside the church are a pair of effigies, once thought to be of the De La Meres, but more likely to be Penrice or Mansels. The church bell is 14th century and inscribed 'Sancta Maria ora pro nobis' (St Mary pray for us). The churchyard is claimed to be haunted by a horse on its hind legs.

In the sea north-east of the church are the 'V' shaped remains of three fish traps which are on the low tide mark, designed to trap fish as the tide recedes. These appear to be more visible at certain times, depending on tides and sands. On the headland are the outlines of Maiden Castle, an Iron Age enclosure.

The beach at Oxwich is part of the Penrice Estate and parking is permitted on the beach. Dogs are allowed on the beach year round but must be kept on a lead during busy summer periods. Behind the beach are the dunes and further back a wetland area and nature reserve.

Oystermouth see Mumbles

Pant-yr-awel *Breezy Hollow*

Pant-yr-awel in the Ogmore Valley lies north-west of Blackmill at the junction with the road from Llangeinor. It is named after a house built in the 17th century and refurbished by Richard Hoare Jenkins in the early 19th century. In the early 20th century it was the site of an Isolation Hospital, the buildings of which now form Blackmill Care Home. In the 1930s council housing had been built on the mountainside and further housing has been added since the Second World War.

There is a Post Office but no other amenities or places of worship.

Parkmill

Parkmill as the name suggests was a mill village set within a park. It once lay within the Parc le Breos, established as a deer park by John de Braose, the Norman Lord of Gower in the early 13th century. Today it lies on the A4118 about a mile north of Three Cliffs Bay.

Entered from the east through the wooded valley of Ilston River, there is the Gower Inn and the West Glamorgan Guides Activity Centre, in the former Ilston Lodge School built in 1876. Stone Mill corn mill was a medieval corn mill, still in use at the start of the 20th century, but now a private house. A mill pond was fed by a leat from the river. On the opposite side of the road once stood the village forge. The village has a shop, Shepherds, whose most famous family member was Don Shepherd the long serving Glamorgan cricketer. Shortly after his retirement from county cricket in the 1970s he was to be seen serving petrol.

Mount Pisgah Congregational chapel was erected in 1822 and rebuilt in 1890. It is now part of the United Reformed Church.

To the north of the main road is the Gower Heritage Centre on the site of a water powered stone and corn mill that has been restored. Further along this road there is a forestry picnic area with pedestrian access to Green Cwm leading to a Neolithic long cairn burial chamber. The cairn has been removed giving access to the restored burial chamber. Some 40 bodies were buried here and carbon dating dates the tomb to 3,800BC though some bones found date back to 11,000BC and it is speculated that these were transferred from the nearby Cat Hole Cave. Cat Hole Cave shows signs of being used in the Palaeolithic period with a cave painting thought to represent a deer dated to 12,500-14,500BP (BP refers to 'Before Present' for radio carbon dating with 'present' being 1950.) though the earliest estimate for habitation is 33,000-32,000BP. There is evidence of use by hunter gatherers during the Mesolithic period and Bronze Age artefacts have also been found.

Opposite the cairn is a well preserved lime kiln, used to produce lime for fertilizer and lime washing walls.

Green Cwm passes through the medieval deer park the limits of its 2000 acres are still visible as an oval through banks ditches and natural boundaries. The park was subsequently divided among a number of farms.

Penclawdd *Head of the Bank*

Penclawdd is famous for its cockles which have been gathered on the mud flats of the Loughor estuary since Roman Times. A large village, it once had three collieries and a copper, tinplate and brass works as well as a quarrying industry. Even the cockle factories have now moved to nearby Crofty, leaving a large village with its promenade overlooking the estuary with a few pleasure boats moored in the old dock area. The village is large enough to have a range of shops, takeaways, a supermarket and a number of public houses.

The church of St Gwynour is situated south of the village in the area known as Blue Anchor. Rebuilt in 1850 by the Swansea architect George E. Strawbridge on the site of a medieval church, St Gwynour's is constructed of blocks of local sandstone. The spire was rebuilt in 1896 and the chancel in 1926. It has north and south transepts which incorporate a vestry and a west porch beneath the tower with its spire. Only the font and a few memorials predate the rebuilding in the interior. The dedication to St Gwynour appears to be unique to Penclawdd and the saint is not listed by Baring-Gould.

Mount Hermon Baptist chapel was built in 1807, but is no longer in use. Trinity Baptist chapel was built in 1803 and rebuilt in 1867 and 1905. Bethel Independent chapel was built in 1816 and rebuilt in 1848, 1870 and 1884. The church-like Tabernacle Welsh Calvinistic Methodist chapel with its tower and spire, was erected in 1836.

Penclawdd was a port until the 1870s and a canal and tramroad were constructed in 1814 to transport coal from mines at Waunarlwydd. The canal however had failed as a commercial enterprise by 1818 and fell into decay.

Penclawdd Copperworks was active in the late 18th and early 19th century but closed in 1811 to be revived between 1848 and 1868 after which the works were used for lead and silver smelting and tinplate. Parts of the factory remain near Station Terrace and the outlines of the works own dock is also evident. The site of the station on the line to Crofty is now a commercial estate while to the east the line of the track runs alongside Gowerton Road.

South of Waun y Felin is the oval outline of an Iron Age hillfort, using the natural rise to the north with a 10ft embankment to the south.

The estuary sands, mud flats and salt marsh provide a home for a variety of wildlife with the Welsh Wetland Centre lying on the north side of the Loughor.

Penllergaer *Head of the Fort*

Penllergaer is situated just south of the M4 and the Swansea East Junction. The village has seen significant expansion in recent years, with new housing developments and an industrial estate to the west of the village. The main Gorseinon Road runs for part along Gorseinon Common, giving an open feel to part of the village.

Carn Goch Common to the south of the village was the site of the Battle of Gower, in which Hywel ap Maredudd defeated a Norman army on New Year's Day 1136. A memorial stone was unveiled to commemorate the battle in 1986.

East of the village was Penllergare House, the home of the Llewelyn family. (The spelling 'Penllergare' was retained from early deeds). The house was demolished in 1961, but the Equatorial Observatory built by John Dillwyn Llewelyn in 1846 remains and is to be restored. This observatory was used by Llewelyn to take one the first photographs of the moon. Llewelyn created one of the finest gardens in Britain to the east of the village and, after years of neglect the Penlergare Trust are to undertake work to restore the gardens which have suffered from the encroachment of the Parc Penllergaer housing development and the M4 motorway. The Trust is to open the terrace gardens, upper lake, waterfall and an old stone bridge known as the Llewelyn Bridge. John Dillwyn Llewelyn as well as being a pioneering photographer (he was a cousin of Fox Talbot) and landscape gardener, invented an electrically powered boat for use on the lake and also designed an orchid house with hot water cascades to provide an environment for non-terrestrial plants. The site of Penllergare House is now occupied by a civic centre for Swansea City Council.

One of the oldest buildings in the village itself is the early 19th century Old Inn, standing near the roundabout. In 1837 the foundation stone was laid for the chapel of ease of St David, the building of which was financed by John Dillwyn Llewelyn. The church eventually became the parish church in 1937. The building is cruciform with a western bellcote and porch and a vestry.

Salem Calvinistic Methodist Chapel and Bethel Congregational Chapels both dating from the early 20th century have disappeared.

Penmaen *Stone Head*

Penmaen is a village located on and to the north of the A4118 west of Parkmill. Standing on the southern slopes of Cefn Bryn which is the spine of the Gower peninsular, it offers views over the channel with Three Cliffs and Oxwich Bays.

The original settlement would appear to have been nearer the coast on what is now Penmaen Burrows. Here there are the remains of St Mary's church. Now just the outline of the walls of a large church some 100ft by 20ft, it was abandoned by 1320. The Norman castle had been abandoned a century earlier. The earthworks remain and excavation showed that there were dry stone walls topped by a wooden structure which was destroyed by fire in 1217. The area later became a rabbit warren with pillow mounds for rabbit farming.

The church of St John the Baptist was built to replace St Mary's but it was substantially rebuilt in 1852-55 by the architect R. K. Penson. There is a double aisled nave, chancel and bellcote and the church has some fine 19th century stained glass.

North-west of the church is Three Cliffs Nursing Home, which occupies the site of the former workhouse.

On Cefn Bryn are three cairns of disputed date possibly Bronze Age but with more modern additions.

North of the village is Parc le Breos Farm, thought to be the site of the former hunting lodge of the Park.

Pennard (also known as Pennarth signifying 'Bear's Head')

The village of Pennard lies on the B4436 and its boundaries take in the larger settlements of Southgate and Sandy Lane south of Parkmill. It would appear that there were originally two distinct villages with Pennard Castle, its church and village lying over a mile to the west of the present village beyond the Pennard Golf Course. This western village was abandoned in 1532 when it was inundated by sand.

Both churches were dedicated to St Mary and were 13th century in origin. The remains of the western church are to the east of the castle in the middle of the golf course and consist mainly of the footings except for the west wall which stands up to eight feet.

The present church has a west tower, nave, chancel with a vestry and south porch. It was renovated in 1847, but retains a number of older features including an 18th century wall board of the Ten Commandments beneath the Royal Coat of Arms.

Pennard Castle is of uncertain date but was thought to have been originally built as a ring work by Henry de Beaumont, 1st Earl of Warwick in the 12th century. The stone structure is late 13th century and probably the work of the De Braose family. According to legend a returning warrior held a large party at the castle to celebrate a victory in battle. In the midst of the festivities lights were seen on the beach and the warriors fuelled by drink went to drive out whoever was invading their party. They found and attacked a group of fairies on the beach dancing in the moonbeams whereupon the fairies said "Stop thy warring ways. Thy canst harm us with thy swords and spears. Cursed shall you and your castle be for spoiling our innocent game!" and suddenly a great sandstorm descended from the sky and engulfed the castle and its village, leaving it in ruins. The castle itself is said to be haunted by a Gwrach-y-rhibyn the Welsh equivalent of the Irish Banshee and anyone spending the night in the ruins is

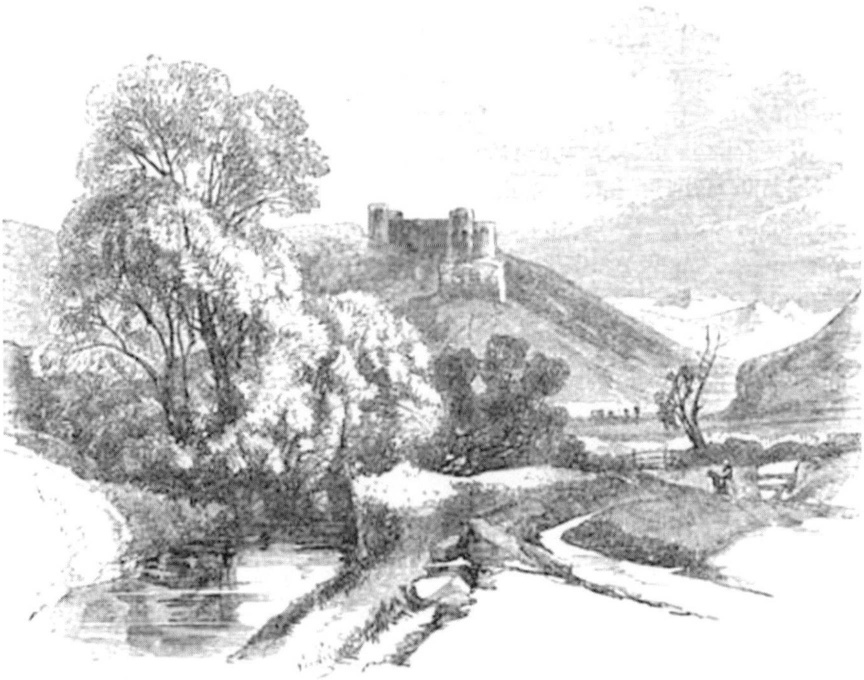

Pennard Castle

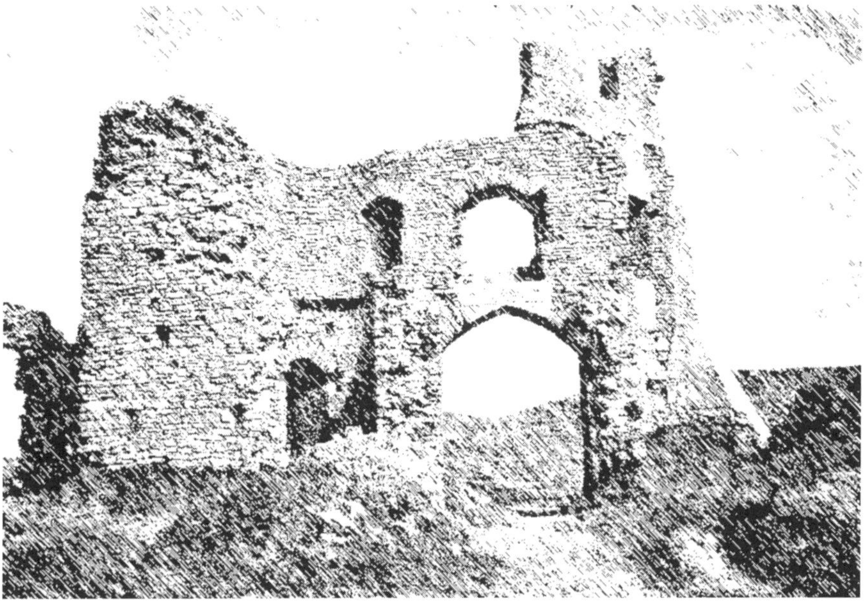

Pennard Castle

condemned to instant madness. The ruins offer a spectacular view over Pennard Pill and Three Cliffs Bay.

To the east on Pwll-Du Head are the overgrown earthworks of an Iron Age promontory fort which excavations have shown was occupied well after the Roman invasion.

Sandy Lane and Southgate are largely 20th century developments, large enough to justify a library and primary school. There is car parking at Southgate between East and West Cliff Roads, giving access to walks along the cliffs and the small sandy beach beneath. Pennard Golf Course is a par 71 links course set above the cliffs. It was established in 1896.

The area is rich in limestone which was used to build the castle and also shipped to Devon and Somerset. In the north of the parish on the northern side of the A4118 is Vennaway Lime Kiln, a well preserved example which would have been supplied by the quarry immediately to the north. Nearby Kilvrough Manor is an 18th century house now used as an outdoor education centre by Oxfordshire schools.

Pen-Rhiw-fawr *Top of the Large Hill*

Surrounded by farmland, Pen-Rhiw-fawr is a hamlet on the road which runs to the west of the main A4068 from Cwm Twrch Isaf to Cwmllynfell. It connects with the road which runs across the Cefn Gwrhyd mountain to Rhyd-y-Fro.

A community of some 75 mixed houses, mainly built over the last century the village has a school and the Rhiwfawr Independent Chapel built in 1876 and rebuilt in 1905. The area to the north of the village has been restored to agricultural use after opencast mining in the 1960s and there were small collieries and pits to the south of the village.

On the road across Cefn Gwrhyd are the remains of a possible ring cairn near the isolated and windswept Gwrhyd Independent Chapel built in 1856 with the chapel house attached.

Penrice

Penrice is today an attractive small village to the north of Oxwich, though it was once the largest village on Gower. It was entitled to a market on Thursday and fairs on the 17th of May, 17th of July, 17th of September, and old St. Andrew's Day, 5th of December. Carlisle in 1811 reported "In the Village of Penrice (formerly a Town) stands the ancient Market Place, where the Pedlers and Hawkers expose their respective goods for sale on the Fair days". The only evidence of the market place today appears to be the base of a market cross in the centre of the green, though it would appear that the green extended past the church. Rose Cottage along the lane was formerly the Rising Sun Inn.

According to Samuel Lewis "This place is thought to have derived its name, signifying "the head of Rhys," from the circumstance of Rhys ab Caradoc ab Iestyn having been defeated and slain here, in defending his territories from the aggression of a party of Norman invaders. According to other authorities, the place is said to have obtained its name from the family of Penrice, who accompanied William the Conqueror into England, and after wards effected a settlement in Gower, in the reign of Edward I". The actual name of the Norman family was de Penres.

The first castle in the village was a ring work topped by wooden staves just west of the village green. It was built by Henry de

Beaumont, 1st Earl of Warwick in 1099. Around 1237 the estate was in the hands of Robert de Penres who built a stone castle, the largest in Gower, to the east of the village. In June 1377, another Robert de Penres was convicted of murdering a woman in Llanstephan, some seven years earlier, and his estates were forfeited and granted to Rhys ap Gruffudd. They were bought back by Robert's son, also Robert, for 500 marks after the death of Rhys's son, yet another Robert, in 1391. In 1394 the castle passed to Sir John de Penres who held Oxwich Castle, but on his death in 1410, having survived capture by Owain Glyndwr, the estates passed to Hugh Mansel who had married Isabella de Penres. The Mansels continued to hold Penrice until 1750, though the other castles were forfeited for a time during the Wars of the Roses. With the improvements to Oxwich Castle by Sir Rice Mansel in the 16th century, the family seat was transferred there and Penrice Castle was leased to William Benet in 1534. The Benet family continued to live in the castle until 1669 though much of it was by then in ruin and indeed it continued to be occupied by tenants into the 18th century.

The Mansels while retaining their estates in Gower had established themselves at Margam Abbey where they built a large mansion. In 1750 the estates passed to the Revd Thomas Talbot of Laycock in Wiltshire. His heir Thomas Mansel Talbot however moved the family seat to a new mansion at Penrice built in the mid 1770s with landscaped gardens. The property is still in the hands of the descendants of the Talbot family.

Penrice Castle is on private land, but a footpath provides views of the ruins.

St Andrew's church dates from the early 12th century, though much restored following a storm in 1720 which removed the roof and further late Victorian work. Cruciform in shape with a west tower, the Penres family granted the church to the Knights Hospitallers of St John at the Slebech Commandery during the time of David, Bishop of St David's (1147-1176). The church was later appropriated to the Hospital of St David at Swansea. In the churchyard is a tombstone with the following inscription: 'To the memory of Mary, wife of James Kavanagh of Penmaen, who was murdered by .... on the 3rd October 1829, aged 75 years', presumably the murderer was never apprehended.

South-west of the village is Sanctuary farm, said to have belonged to the manor of Millwood, or St John's, the property of the Knights Hospitallers.

Pentrebach *Little Village*

Pentrebach is a hamlet north of Pontardulais on the road to Garnswllt on the east bank of the River Loughor. There are just a few houses along the narrow high hedged road. The White Springs Coarse Fishery has a number of lakes.

Above the village, on Graig Fawr, is a cairnfield of unknown date. The numerous cairns are grass covered and only a foot in height.

Pen-y-fai *End of the Plain*

Pen-y-fai, a little over a mile north of Bridgend, is a former estate village that has expanded dramatically since the end of the Second World War. Originally built to serve the Court Colman estate with Court Colman Manor built in 1776 for the Llewellyn family. The major part of the modern village is built on top of the hill overlooking the Ogmore Valley and Pen-y-fai Common.

Court Colman Manor is now a country hotel with one of the finest Indian restaurants in Wales. The Pheasant, formerly an old farmhouse, is a large inn at the bottom of the hill. The New Inn half way up the hill is now closed and converted to a private dwelling called The Old Tavern.

A pound for animals straying on the common was to be found opposite the turning for Llangewydd at the top of the hill.

All Saints Church was built in 1903, land and finance donated by Mr R. W. Llewellyn, though there is evidence that the dedication was to be to St Colman. The church is cruciform with a crossing tower, a feature usually seen only in larger churches. Much older than the church is Smyrna Baptist Chapel, built in 1718 and rebuilt in 1838.

The village has a shop and primary school.

The Dogs' Trust rehoming kennels is now situated in the village, on the Court Colman estate.

East of the village was the Angelton County Lunatic Asylum. The hospital has been demolished and a housing development now occupies the site and grounds. Further east, the Glanrhyd Hospital provides for in-patient mental health care.

Pilton and Pilton Green

These hamlets are little more than farmsteads on the B4247 to Rhossili, though at Pilton Green there was the Emmanuel Independent Chapel, built in 1821 and rebuilt in 1874 but now a private dwelling. The main point of interest is that Pilton Green gives access via a footpath to the cliffs of south-west Gower with spectacular views and the famous Paviland Cave.

In 1823 Revd Buckland discovered a skeleton covered in red ochre and ceremonially buried with ivory ornaments and perforated sea shells in the Goat's Hole Cave. He identified the skeleton as the 'Red Lady' of Paviland. Buckland was a professor of Geology at Oxford and in a time before Darwin did not contemplate anything older than the date of Biblical creation and attributed the male skeleton to that of a female Roman prostitute. Radiocarbon dating however has dated the skeleton to around 33,000BP and recent research in the cave indicates human presence up to 50,000 years, well before the last Ice Age in Britain when the cave would have been some 70 miles inland. The cave can be accessed with some difficulty at low tide. There are a number of caves in the vicinity, including the Hound's Hole and Fox Hole Caves. Paviland Cave is named after Paviland Manor.

The cliffs are littered with the earthworks of Iron Age promontory and hill forts.

Pitton

Pitton is a hamlet east of Rhossili where there is a car park giving access to the beautiful Mewslade Bay, which has a good beach except at high tide. Access to the beach is by a path through a wooded valley owned by the National Trust. It can be muddy and is not suitable for pushchairs or wheelchairs.

To the north of the B4247 there is Pitton Mill, a former corn mill with overshot wheel powered by the stream flowing from Rhossili Down. Pitton Wesleyan Methodist Chapel was built in 1887.

Pontlliw

Pontlliw was originally a ribbon development along the A48 between Penllergaer and Pontardulais, but new housing developments have led to a larger, more widespread village.

Industry came early to Pontlliw with the Lliw Forge established around 1740. The forge used water power from a pond fed by the race from Lliw Corn Mill further up the Afon Lliw. The forge continued to operate into the 20th century as did the flour mill which has now been converted to a private dwelling. Today there is a furniture factory in the village.

Carmel Baptist Chapel after which Carmel Road was named, was built in 1834, and rebuilt in 1851 and 1885. Peniel Independent Chapel was built in 1908 but is now a private house. There was also an Apostolic Church in Woodfield Avenue which is now a private house.

St Anne's mission Church is a 20th century temporary building under the parish of Penllergaer.

There is a primary school, village hall and a number of small shops together with two pubs, The Buck Inn and The Castle Inn.

Pontrhydyfen *Bridge of the Wagon Ford*

Pontrhydyfen is famous as the birthplace of Richard Walter Jenkins, better known as Richard Burton, in 1925.

Situated in the Afan Valley above Cwmafan, at the confluence of the Afan Pelenna and the River Afan there is a road bridge and above it a viaduct which carried a tramroad and a leat carrying water to drive the waterwheels at the Oakwood blast furnaces. The viaduct which is 75 feet high and 459 feet long was built in 1825 and today is used by cyclists and pedestrians. There is a ten-arch railway viaduct built in 1898 to carry the South Wales Mineral Railway Junction line of the Port Talbot Railway and Dock company. There used to be a fourth bridge carrying the railway from Glyncorrwg.

The village is in two parts, with Oakwood on one side of the river. In 1824 John Reynolds built an iron works with two blast furnaces and coke ovens. He built the viaduct and the tram road to the docks at Aberavon together with the viaduct and 60 houses. Reynolds sold out in 1838 and all trace of the iron works which were situated in what is now forestry, east of Afan Valley Road, has disappeared.

The village has a mini supermarket and post office and the three storey Miners Arms which is home to Pontrhydyfen rugby Club. There is a primary school and rugby ground.

St John's Church was built in 1913, replacing an earlier church of 1883. It was paid for by Miss Talbot of Margam Castle and consisted of a nave, chancel, western bellcote and southern transept and porch. It is now a five bedroom private dwelling. Bethel Baptist Chapel in Aqueduct Terrace was originally built in 1850, but substantially renovated in 1903. Built in the Classical style, it is unusual in that extending up from the main facade is a wall, concealing the gable end roof. It was here that the memorial service for Richard Burton was held. It is no longer in use as a chapel. Jerusalem Calvinistic Methodist Chapel was built in 1824 and rebuilt in 1845 and 1876.

The village has seen only modest expansion and is today a commuter village for Neath and Port Talbot. There are walks in the forests that surround the village as well as along the rivers.

Pontycymer *Bridge on the Confluence*

Pontycymer, also spelt Pontycymmer is a former mining village in the Garw Valley. There were two collieries, Ffaldau and Braich y Cymmer covered under the Blaengarw article. The 1876 Ordnance Survey map shows hardly a house with a tree lined valley floor and the railway running through. By 1899 the scene had changed dramatically with the streets and houses much as they are today.

Pontycymer was the commercial centre for the Garw Valley as witnessed by the number of shops still present in Oxford Street. It was also home to Garw Grammar School, whose most infamous pupil was Howard Marks, the drug dealer and subject of the film *Mr Nice.*

With the influx of population came the churches, chapels and public houses.

The first church was St Theodore's, built in 1899 and closed in 1964. A Welsh mission church followed, becoming All Saints Church but closed in 1949. Another Welsh church St David's was built in 1910 and linked with St Cein's at Llangeinor. It is still open for worship. Brick built on almost a north south axis, it has a nave, chancel and northern bellcote.

Noddfa Baptist Chapel, on the corner of Chapel Street on the western side of the river, was built in 1878 and rebuilt in 1916 it has now been demolished. Bethel Calvinistic Methodist Chapel was built in 1885 but appears to be no longer in use. The Tabernacle Independent Chapel, on Meadow Street, was built in 1890 and is still in use. Bethany Calvinistic Methodist Chapel, on Adare Street, has been demolished. Zion Baptist Chapel on Oxford Street was built in 1885 and rebuilt in 1905. It has now been demolished. The United Reformed Church on the corner of Meadow Street and Alexandra Road was built in 1895 as the Wesleyan English chapel and is still in use.

There are numerous clubs in the village together with the Ffaldau Arms and the Squirrel Hotel. The Royal Hotel is now home to the Garw Athletic Football Club.

The valley today has returned to its former state, coal mining has gone but the people and houses remain. There is limited industry in the valley which has become a commuter area for the Bridgend area. The west of the valley is forested as is the eastern side, though to a much lesser extent.

Pont-y-rhyl

Pont-y-rhyl is a small village in the Garw Valley between Llangeinor and Pontycymer, just south of the confluence of the Garw and Garw Fechan rivers. Known as Pont-y-rhyll in 1877, the village had a station by 1900. St. Mary's chapel of ease to St. Theodore's, in Pontycymer was built above the main street though this was closed in 1986 and is now a private house. There was also Carmel Independent Chapel and a school. The Braich y Cymmer Hotel was originally called the Garw Junction Hotel. A tramway led down from small scale coal levels on Craig-ddu, closed by 1900. The village takes its name from the Rhyll and Coed y Rhyll areas to the north of the village, between the two Garw Rivers, though the spelling is now 'Rhyl'. There is a recreation area in the valley, shared with Lluest on the opposite side of the valley. With only limited development this is one of the more attractive mining valley villages.

Port Eynon

Port Eynon is a popular beach village in south-west Gower. Thought to have been named after an 11th century Welsh prince, it was once a thriving port. The village had an oyster-fishery with the catch shipped to Bristol, as well as a trade in limestone engaging some twenty vessels of between thirty to sixty tons. The remains of the harbour wall can just be seen at the south-western end of the beach offshore from the extensive remains of the old salt works. The salt house dates from the 16th century but was closed in 1650, though partially restored for display in the 1980s. Sea water was evaporated in pans heated by coal fired furnaces, leaving the sea salt which was then stored in the salt house.

St Cattwg's Church was founded in the 6th century. The dedication is subject to differing spellings, Cattwg, Cadocus or Cadoc. The present building dates from the 12th century with a Norman doorway, but the building was much altered in 1861 when it was enlarged. There is a nave, chancel and western double bellcote. There are memorials to three members of the lifeboat crew who died in 1916 and a window in the nave by Celtic Studios also commemorates the RNLI. The Lifeboat Station was moved across the bay to Horton in 1919.

Around Port Eynon Point is Culver Hole, a natural sea cave which has been walled up and used as a dovecote. The wall is some 50 feet high and inside there are 30 tiers of nesting boxes. There has been speculation as to its use for smuggling which was rife in the village and there is a legend that there was a passage from Culver Hole to the Salt House.

The village today has a Youth Hostel, a number of beach front shops as well as the Ship Inn and the Culver House Hotel. There are four holiday caravan and or camping parks signifying the popularity of this part of Gower.

Pricetown

Pricetown is a former mining village in the Ogmore Valley, situated between Ogmore Vale and Nantymoel. Although shown as a separate village, it houses the Nantymoel Post Office and primary school. It was also home to the massive Nantymoel Workmen's Hall and

Institute, built in 1902. It was enlarged in 1910 and further work was carried out in the 1930s which converted the front of the building and installed a cinema with sound system. Mining subsidence resulted in the need for further work in 1952. It is now known as the Berwyn Centre, operated by Bridgend County Council as a leisure and arts centre.

The only place of worship still in use is Bethany Calvinistic Methodist Chapel on Hill Street, built in 1896 and rebuilt in 1905. Soar Independent Chapel on John Street was built in 1803. It has been replaced by a private dwelling. Hope Independent Chapel was built in 1898 and is now a furniture and carpet store. A mission church was built on Ogwy Street but has been demolished.

Pyle *Welsh Y Pîl*

Pyle is located on the A48 between Laleston and Margam. The name has the same derivation as 'pill', meaning a tidal inlet, which was probably the case prior to the inundation of sand in the 15th century. It was established when the sands invaded Kenfig and the church of St James was built in 1471, using stone from the former Kenfig church of the same name. Development was slow. The 1877 map shows a few cottages around Pyle cross, the Pisgah chapel, the church, vicarage and three public houses, the Pyle Inn, the Old House and the Walnut Tree.

The Pyle Inn was a large late 18th century coaching inn with up to 40 beds. According to Rees it had the appearance of an elegant gentleman's residence. Among its clientele was said to be Lord Nelson and Isambard Kingdom Brunel. It lost its licence in 1886 following the death of the landlord and was converted into flats before being demolished in 1959. The site is now occupied by Longlands Close. The Old House survives as Ye Olde Wine House on the A48. The Walnut Tree is on Pisgah Road.

There was some development along the road to Kenfig Hill by 1900, and in the period running up to the Second World War there was a housing estate built to the west of the A48. Post war development however has seen a large increase in housing and commercial development, aided by proximity and access to the M4 and the resulting decline in traffic on the A48. The village now boasts a large supermarket, a parade of small shops, a junior school, and recreational facilities. On the outskirts is the Village Farm Industrial Estate.

St James Church stands alongside the A48, a Grade I listed building. It dates from 1471 and there was a dispute as to which church, Mawdlam or Pyle should be the parish church. St James has a nave and chancel with a three storey tower and south porch. It was renovated in 1876-7 by the Llandaff Diocesan architect, John Prichard.

Pisgah Baptist Chapel was built in 1835, rebuilt in 1857 and again in 1912. Mount Zion English Baptist Chapel was built in 1926. St Joseph's Roman Catholic Church on Pisgah Street is 20th century.

East of Pyle is Stormy Down, the site of a Norman motte and bailey castle built by Geoffrey Sturmi around 1150. The original name was Sturmiestown and there was once a chapel. The land was in the possession of Margam Abbey by 1166. In 1940 an RAF airfield was established with a grass runway. It was used for armament training and was later, in the war, used by French and subsequently American forces. It was abandoned as an airfield in 1944, though continued in use for some years with a large radar aerial. It is now the site of a concrete works and a proposed wind farm.

The officer commanding No 7 Bombing and Gunnery School at Stormy in 1940 was Acting Wing Commander James Ira Thomas 'Taffy' Jones DSO, MC, DFC & Bar, and MM. While flying an unarmed Hawker Henley near Swansea he attacked a German Junkers JU88 bomber with a flare pistol, so effectively that the Junkers broke off its bombing mission.

Resolven

Resolven is a village in the Vale of Neath, south-west of Glyn Neath. The derivation of the name is unclear, but one theory is that it is a corruption of Rhys Sylfan, Rhys ab Iestyn having been granted the land after the Conquest and Sylfan meaning a place to gaze. Another theory is that it derives from Rhos-haf-lyn – Moor of the Summer Lake.

Samuel Lewis described Resolven as a township situated "near the left bank of the river Neath, where the mountains are lofty and rugged, and their declivities and the glens well covered with timber. Solven hill is an elevated mountain in the hamlet, at the western base of which, overlooking the Neath, are the remains of Glyn Castle; the streams that flow into that river through the glens of the mountains form many pleasing cascades. Here is a chapel of ease to the parochial church; and two Sunday schools, containing about 50 children, are supported by subscription".

Resolven had been a grange of the Cistercians at Neath Abbey, which was apparently attacked by the locals in 1227.

Melincwrt Ironworks started in 1708 in the valley of the Melin Court Brook which drove the waterwheel powering the blast furnace. Originally charcoal fired, it converted to coke at the end of the 18th century before closing in 1808.

Coal mining as a major industry started in Resolven in 1840 when James Witton Lyon Esq. opened the Resolven Colliery in Cwm Clydach. Lyon's Place, a terrace of 18 houses was built to accommodate miners and remained in the ownership of successive colliery proprietors until sold by the National Coal Board to tenants. The Resolven Colliery was followed in the 1850s by Rheola Colliery and in 1875 by Glyncastle Colliery, both in Cwm Clydach. At their peak some 900 men were employed. Rheola, closed in 1921, to be reopened by D. W. Evans in 1952 when it continued in operation until 1994. Resolven and Glyncastle Collieries had closed by 1965.

Glyn Castle above Cwm Clydach is a small gentry house of 'renaissance' style built around 1700, probably on the foundations of an older property.

Resolven was created a parish in 1850 when the former chapel of ease was replaced by St David's Church in Neath Road. The church has a nave, chancel, vestry and south-western bellcote. The chancel has a stained glass window of 1869 depicting the crucifixion by Joseph Bell & Sons. Windows in the nave are from 1950. The church has recently undergone renovation. The church hall is in the centre of the village next to the War Memorial.

Melin-Cwrt Independent Chapel on Waterfall Road was built in 1800 and rebuilt 1850-54. Situated just above the waterfall, a replacement chapel, Jerusalem was built in Neath Road in the village in 1875 and refurbished in 1902. Sardis Baptist Chapel was built in 1864, and a new chapel built alongside in 1904 in an unusual mixture of Romanesque and Art Deco styles.

The beautiful Melincourt waterfall is one of the highest in South Wales and has been a tourist attraction since the 18th century. Leigh's Guide described falls as: "a beautiful cascade formed by the river Cledaugh or Cleddau, which is here precipitated about eighty feet. The adjacent crags are richly clothed with foliage, and as an enclosed scene it may be considered unrivalled".

Tabernacl Calvinistic Methodist Chapel is a new building at the corner of Lyon's Place, replacing an early 20th century chapel on the site and the 1868 Tabernacl Chapel in Tanyrhiw Road. Bethania Baptist Chapel was built in 1858 and rebuilt in 1875. Bethel Free Baptist Chapel was built after the Second World War but has been demolished.

Above the village, adjacent to the Coed Morgannwg Way is Carn Clagau, a Bronze Age cairn, some 30 feet in diameter but less than two feet high. There are also earthworks of an Iron Age settlement and Roman marching camp above the Melin Court Brook.

The village today has an array of small shops and a Costcutter supermarket, primary school and library. There is the Vaughan Arms, Resolven Miners' Welfare and Resolven Rugby Club, while across the river and Heads of the Valleys road is the Farmers' Arms. The large Workman's Institute building in which the Miners' Welfare club is based is in an interesting 1920s style, and was used as a 750 seat cinema and public hall as well as having its own library, reading room and billiard hall. Employment is provided in an industrial estate south-west of the village.

The surrounding scenery is now reverting back to that described by Lewis above. Resolven Mountain is tree clad and the Neath Canal above Resolven with its locks and aqueducts is navigable for four miles. Melin Court Waterfall is particularly attractive. There are walks and trails in the valley and on the mountains with the Coed Morgannwg Way walking trail.

Reynoldston

Reynoldston is today a fairly large village situated on the southern slopes of Cefn Bryn in the west of the Gower. The views from Cefn Bryn are a particular attraction and being on the cross roads between north and south Gower the area is popular in summer. The village is thought to take its name from Reginald de Breos, the lord of the manor who established the church of St George in the 13th century.

The old village was small, centred around the church and village green, but expanded in the early 19th century with a ribbon development encroaching onto the common land. More recent development has taken place to the north of the church and into Lower Reynoldston.

St George's Church was rebuilt in 1867 on the original site with only a lancet in the south wall remaining from the original. It has a nave, chancel, north transept, western double bellcote, south porch and vestry.

The Wesleyan Methodist chapel was founded in 1869.

Reynoldston possessed its own brewery in the 19th century, situated to the south of the Lower Green, as well as a post office, blacksmith and hotel. The post office and hotel, the King Arthur, remain.

Above the village on Cefn Bryn is King Arthur's Stone, a Neolithic burial chamber dating from 2500BC and in the 16th century was regarded as one of the three mighty achievements of ancient Britain, the others being Stonehenge and Silbury Hill. The capstone is immense, weighing 25 tons though prior to 1693 it was even larger. A local miller is said to have cut a piece from the capstone to use as a millstone, only to find that at 10 tons it was impossible to move. Other explanations given for the break in the capstone are that St David smashed it with his sword because it was used by druids or that it was split by lightning. Whatever the explanation, the broken piece remains on the ground alongside the chamber. The capstone was probably deposited by glaciers in the Ice Age and the builders of the tomb dug under it, creating two tombs with the insertion of upright supporting stones.

There are a number of cairns and standing stones around the village and an Iron Age hillfort was situated to the east of the King Arthur Hotel, though not marked on the Ordnance Survey map.

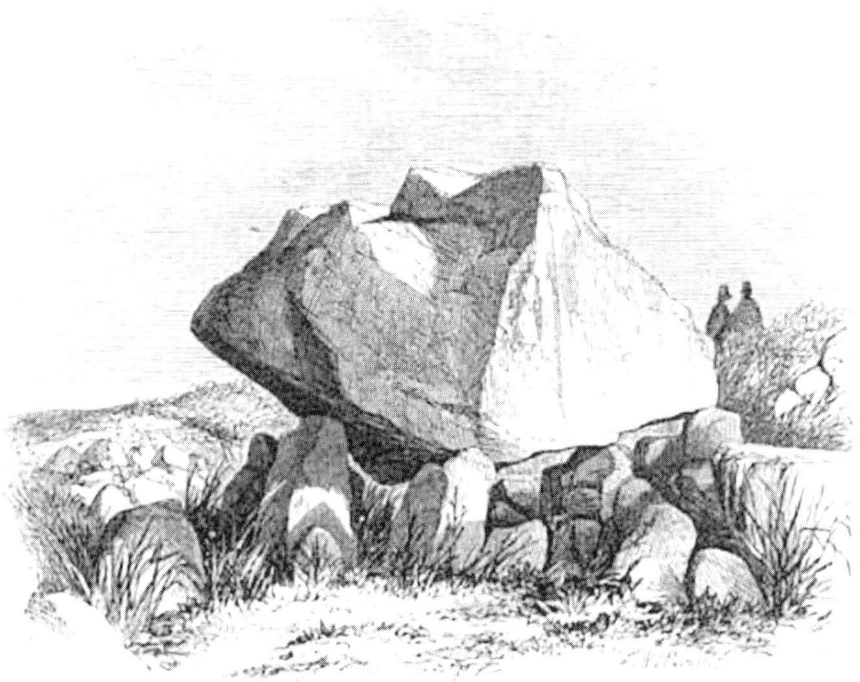

Arthur's Stone

In 1763 "John William was indicted for feloniously altering the ear marks of a certain white-horned ewe sheep, the property of Owen Punner, at Reynaldstone."

Rhos *Moor*

Originally a ribbon development along the A474 Neath to Pontardawe road, Rhos has developed into a sizeable village over the last 50 years with developments to the west and north-east of the main road.

The Primrose Colliery was developed in the mid 19th century near what are now Primrose Lane and Primrose House. In October 1858 fourteen men and boys, and seven horses were suffocated from the fumes of an underground engine boiler. Mining continued under various owners, with over 300 men employed, until 1908 after which it was maintained as a pumping station for the Tareni Colliery until that closed in 1949.

The village has a primary school and the Smiths Arms, a post office and hairdressers.

Ebenezer Independent Chapel on the A474 was built in 1904.

Rhossili

The little village of Rhossili at the south-western tip of the Gower peninsular is justly famous for the spectacular scenery of its bay and the promontory of Worm's Head. The Bay was voted in the top ten beaches in the world in a 2013 survey.

Rhossili was occupied in the Bronze Age as shown by the cairns on Rhossili Down to the north of the present village. There are the Iron Age promontory forts of Old Castle Fort overlooking the Bay and Lewes Castle overlooking Fall Bay south of the village.

In the middle of the 19th century limestone was quarried locally and there were 50 men employed in the trade.

In the 13th century part of the village was on what is now the beach and is thought to have been abandoned in the 14th century as the sands encroached. It is thought that the original church was located in what are now dunes and the church of St Mary the Virgin was built around 1200. The carved Norman doorway is a particularly fine example and there is a scratched sundial which may have come from the earlier church. It is conjectured that the now buried church was dedicated to St Sulien or St Sili, giving the village its name of St Sili's Heath. The tower is fortified with a saddleback roof. There are three bells in the tower dating from 1893. There is a Chancel, nave and south porch. On the south side of the chancel there is a 14th century 'leper's window', allowing lepers to view church services without entering the church. The chancel is out of line with the nave, clearly shown on the refurbishment plans and known as a 'weeping chancel'. The church was granted to the Knights Hospitallers of St John around 1230. The church was altered in the Victorian era when Ewen Christian the architect supervised the refurbishment 1890-91. There are some painted heraldic shields from the 18th century, some recently repainted. Among the memorials in the church is one with an Antarctic scene in memory of Edgar Evans who died on the ill-fated

Terra Nova Expedition of Captain Scott to the South Pole in 1912. Petty Officer Evans was born in the nearby hamlet of Middleton.

There is a hotel and large car park catering for the summer visitors. There are two principal attractions, Worm's Head and the Bay.

Worm's Head is a promontory of carboniferous limestone accessible at low tide, consisting of the Inner, Middle and Outer Heads separated by rocks with the Devil's Bridge, a collapsed sea cave connecting the two halves of the Middle Head. Visitors are warned that the Heads are cut off as the tide rises. The Inner head has the remains of and Iron Age defended enclosure.

"Worm's Head extends over a mile out to sea, and in the furthest rock is the Blowhole, a narrow cleft about a foot long and three-quarters of an inch wide, on the hillside opposite to the seaward mouth of the cavern. The noise made by the wind driven out through this aperture when the waves rush in below is astounding, and can be heard, it is affirmed, seven miles off. The country people call the Blowhole the 'Rhosilly Barometer'." Baring-Gould. Barber offers another description: "Near the extremity of the point is a cleft in the

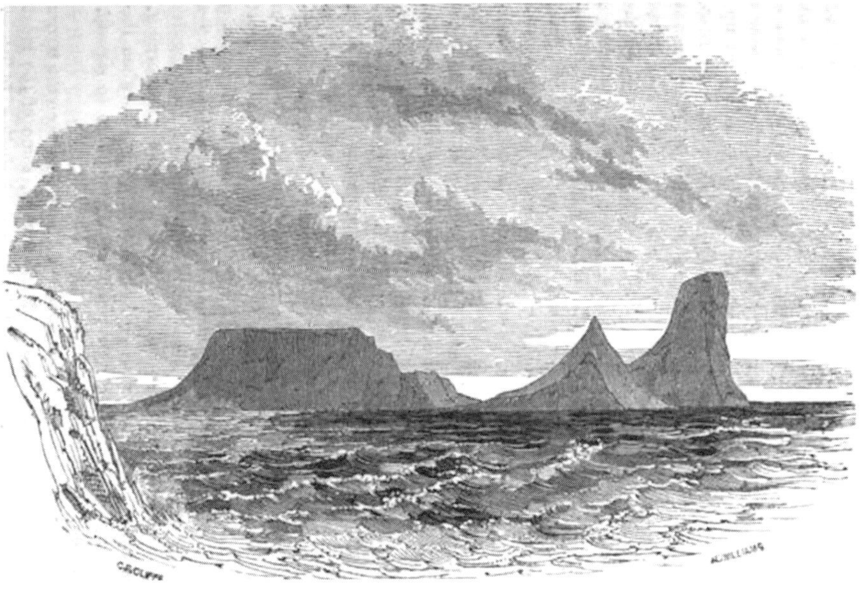

Worm's Head

ground, in which if dust or sand be thrown, it will be returned back into the air; and a person applying his ear to the crevice will hear a deep noise, like the blowing of a large pair of bellows: this effect is reasonably attributed to the concussions of the waves of the sea in the cavernous hollows of the cliff."

Rhossili Bay stretches for three miles and faces due west. It is celebrated for its surfing, particularly towards the northern end. On the beach are remains of a number of wooden ships with timbers visible at low tide. One is thought to be the Helvetia, which sank on 1st November, 1887.

Baring-Gould Relates: "Great interest has for many years existed in Gower relative to the wreck of a Spanish galleon, supposed to have been that conveying to England the dower of Catherine de Braganza. The tradition remained that the vessel had gone down in Rhosilly Bay, and it was a saying among the people that treasure was there for him who would dig for it. One day in 1833 four men of Rhosilly, having observed that there had been a great shifting of the sands after a gale, went to the beach to seek for the hidden treasure, and hit quickly on a quantity of dollars; but the tide rose and overflowed the place. However, they continued digging till the water became too deep. To mark the spot they stuck a quarryman's bill in the sand, with a string tied to it and a bit of cork for a buoy; but on their return next day the mark was gone, and it is supposed that no one ever struck upon this particular spot again. The affair, however, soon got wind, and a number of people flocked to the sands from the neighbouring villages, and much quarrelling and fighting ensued. A large number of dollars was found, all of silver, dating from 1625-39."

In 1807, The Cambrian newspaper of March 7th recorded: "The tides of late having receded much further than usual, the wreck of a vessel has appeared, which was lost there about fifty years ago, and a cask of iron wire was last week recovered. A short distance from the same spot about 12 lbs. of Spanish dollars and half-dollars, of the date 1625, have been found amongst the sand."

Smuggling was rife in the area. Baring-Gould again: "A few hundred yards behind Rhosilly Parsonage may be seen the remains of a smugglers' hiding-place, of very ingenious character. At the back of the rectory is Rhosilly Down, rising some 600 feet above the sea. From this ridge a little stream flows, and about half-way between the source and the foot of the hill the brook runs through a debris of stones of various sizes. This is actually the remains of a cellar constructed in smuggling days under the bed of the rivulet there was a slight jump in the side of the mountain, and over this the water shot in a short cascade. The smugglers, with great ingenuity, taking advantage of this, excavated here a large underground cellar, and when it was finished led the stream over the top of it, and made the entrance, which was closed with a few large slabs, immediately under the waterfall. When they desired to enter and fill the cave with new goods, or to discharge its contents, they turned the stream aside. This hiding-place remained undiscovered, till some years ago, after heavy rain, the structure was burst abroad by the force of the water."

Around the area are a number of old lime kilns, used to burn lime for fertilizing the fields and as a lime wash for houses.

Sarn *Paved Road*

Sarn is a village north of the M4 near Bridgend incorporating Bryncoch. Apart from a few houses on Sarn Hill, Sarn was a 1930s housing estate, much increased post war and with further modern housing developments built on the outskirts. There is a community centre, library and a supermarket, but no school or place of worship. It is served by Sarn railway station on the Maesteg to Bridgend line.

Seven Sisters *(Welsh name Blaendulais)*

Seven Sisters is named after the colliery started in 1872 when the daughter of David Bevan of the Evans Bevan mining company dug the first sod of the colliery. The colliery was named Seven Sisters, because David Bevan had one son and seven daughters and the village took the colliery name.

The village is situated in the upper Dulais valley between Crynant and Onllwyn. It stretches for more than two miles with distinct areas. At its heart was the original Seven Sisters Colliery, the site of which is now a park with relics of the mining industry alongside sheltered accommodation. Opposite is one of two terraces of single storey miners' cottages dating from the early days of the village. There are also shops and takeaways.

The Neath and Brecon Railway had a station but the line is now used for freight only.

Seven Sisters Colliery operated until 1963 employing up to 760 men. Until nationalization it remained in the ownership of the Evans-Bevan company. In 1943 it was used for the film *The Silent Village*, although the village featured was Cwmgiedd across the county border in Breconshire. Five men lost their lives in an underground explosion in 1907.

A mile south of Seven Sisters Colliery the Dillwyn Colliery was opened in 1884 by David Thomas and after a number of owners was purchased by the Evans Bevan company. It employed up to 430 men and closed in1966.

Close to Dillwyn was Brynteg Colliery, opened by Evans-Bevan in 1878. It employed up to 550 men and was closed in 1954 though licences were granted for two private collieries to mine in the area.

As the mining industry grew, so did the village with a mix of housing. The north-eastern end of the village has views over the moorland. New housing is still taking place though there is little industry in the immediate area.

With the influx of workers came the church and chapels. Soar Congregational Chapel was built in 1878 and rebuilt in 1901, Ebenezer Independent Chapel was situated opposite Brynteg and is now a private house, Soar Congregational Chapel was built in 1878, rebuilt in 1901, Olivet Pentecostal Chapel stood on Mary Street, Seion Calvinistic Methodist Chapel was built in 1890 and rebuilt in 1905 but is no longer in use and Salem Baptist Chapel was built in 1899 and then rebuilt in 1911. St Mary's Church was built in 1911 designed by the Neath architect J. Cook-Rees. A large church with a triple aisled nave and chancel, it has a Sanctus bellcote. The east window is by Clayton and Bell and a beautiful work of art. Dating from 1921 it depicts the adoration of the shepherds and wise men. Fire, set by vandals, damaged the church in 2010, but the church celebrated its centenary a year later.

The village has its Miners Welfare club, contained in the Miners' Welfare Hall of 1926 which had a 620 seat cinema. The Welfare also provided an open air swimming pool (now filled in) and playing fields.

The village is well supplied with rugby and football pitches and has a golf driving range. The Bryndulais Inn in Church Road is at the opposite end of the village to the Miners' Welfare.

The Roman road, Sarn Helen ran to the east of the village and there is a banked and ditched rectangular enclosure thought to be a small Roman fort. In the forestry east of the village are the Bronze Age Cwm Irfon standing stones. There are also the Carn Cornel Bronze Age Cairns south of the village and the Twyn Eithinog Cairns to the west on Mynydd-Y-Drum of an unknown age.

Skewen

Skewen today with a population of 8,500 is a large village to the west of Neath. It borders the M4 and the A465 Heads of the Valleys road making it an attractive village for commuters. It is served by the main Swansea to Cardiff railway line which bisects the village. As befits a population of this size it has an array of shops and banks though the larger supermarkets are outside its boundary. The name is thought to derive from either 'Is-cae-ywen', below the field of yew-trees or 'Ysgawen', the Welsh for elder wood, a tree which abounds in the vicinity.

Skewen has an industrial heritage. The Crown Copperworks, located to the east of the A465 dual carriageway, was in existence by 1797, built by the Rose Copper Company of Birmingham. After 1886 the works were adapted for zinc smelting and in the 1920s the plant produced a patented coal product.

There were a number of coal mines in and around the village, owned by the Main Colliery Company which had a number of pits, including the Dynevor Main, Brithdir and Melyn. Mining had ceased by 1939.

The village is home to the Welsh Museum of Fire, with a collection of old fire fighting equipment and fire engines. Operated by the Wales Area Fire Engine Restoration Society it is open on Wednesdays and Saturdays by prior appointment and has a selection of fire engines on display from the Victorian era to the 1970s.

Perhaps the most striking aspect of Skewen is the large number of chapels still in use as the following list reveals. Ebenezer Methodist Chapel was built in 1835, rebuilt 1859, 1881 and 2012. Gorphwysfa Calvinistic Methodist Chapel was built in 1843 by the architect E. Harris, and then rebuilt in 1893. St John's Terrace Chapel, built in 1850, was opposite Gorphwysfa, but is no longer in existence. Horeb Baptist Chapel was built in 1868. The United Methodist Church was stone built before 1918. The Church of Latter Day Saints in Dynevor Road is a modern timber building. The Free Mission Independent Chapel was built after 1918. Salem Calvinistic Methodist Chapel, or Apostolic Church was built in 1919. Tabernacl Welsh Independent Chapel was built in 1842 and rebuilt in 1859 and 1897. Y Capel, Calvinistic Methodist Chapel was built before 1918. Calfaria Welsh Baptist Chapel was built in 1893. Bethania Independent Chapel was stone built in 1908. Hermon Welsh Calvinistic Methodist Chapel was built in 1897. Mount Pleasant Baptist Chapel was built in 1902 but has been demolished and replaced by housing.

The parish church of St John the Baptist was originally dedicated to St John and St Mary the Virgin according to plans drawn up in 1849 for the new church. Designed under the supervision of John Prichard, Richard Cook Saunders drew up the initial plans but the final design was by Egbert Moxham. The church stands on a hill overlooking the lower Neath valley. It has an additional aisle, nave, chancel, vestry, southern porch and western bellcote. The Mission Church of All Saints, built in 1834 in Woodlands Road, has been demolished and new housing built on the site. St Mary's church in Villiers Road was demolished at the end of 2012 with a new church being built on the site of the former red brick building which had small north and south transepts and an apse.

The village has primary schools and pubs including, The Crown, The Miners and The Colliers.

Slade

Slade is a small secluded hamlet on a no through road west of Oxwich Bay. There is a footpath leading to the Coastal Path and to Sands Bay, but no car parking.

Tai'rgwaith *(can be translated as works houses)*

Tai'rgwaith is a small village to the north of Gwaun Cae Gurwen. The church of St David was built in 1913 as a mission church and is of a wooden construction under a slate roof with a western bellcote and porch. The other feature of interest in this village is the trotting track which stages regular harness races.

The area to the north and east of the village has been the site of opencast coal mining and this has led to the reopening of the mineral railway from Ammanford. There is a rail loading area adjacent to the trotting track.

Three Crosses

Three Crosses is an inland village at the eastern end of the Gower. Its name, originally Y Crwys, is derived from the triangular road structure giving three cross roads.

The village is not mentioned in Lewis's *Topographical Dictionary* of 1833, but grew up to service a number of small coal mines in the area. All signs of mining have long disappeared and Three Crosses is a commuter village for Swansea. There is a mix of housing, a primary school and the Skinners Arms.

A Welsh Independent chapel was built in 1700 a mile south-west of the village on the Cilonnen Road near the site of the Whitewalls coal mine but is now in ruins. It was replaced by the large Crwys Independent Chapel, built in the centre of the village in 1788, rebuilt in 1831, modified in 1851 and subsequently rebuilt in 1875 and further enlarged in 1911. It would appear that the original chapel on the site was added to with the new chapel at right angles built in 1875.

Tircoed Forest Village

Tircoed Forest Village is a new village built from the 1980s to the north of the M4 Penllergaer Services. It is accessible from the A48 and has a village store, hall and playing fields. Tircoed means woodland.

Tondu

Originally Ton Ithel Du or The Fort of Black Ithel, Tondu is a village with a significant industrial heritage.

There had been coal mining in the area for some years and in 1828 a railway line was constructed to take coal from the Llynfi Valley, via

Tondu to Porthcawl. Originally the wagons were horse drawn and the journey took six and a half hours. In 1836, Sir Robert Price, a Herefordshire M.P. and son of Sir Uvedale Price the author of the concept of the 'Picturesque' acquired land at Tondu Farm from the liquidator of the John Bedford estate. Bedford had attempted to create an ironworks at Cefn Cribwr, but, more concerned with theory than business, had failed. Sir Robert Price traded as the Glamorgan Coal and Iron Company and his business was boosted by the discovery of extensive reserves of black-band ironstone six miles away at Maesteg in 1843. He developed the Tywith coal and ironstone mine near Nantyffyllon but in the early 1850s iron prices slumped and Sir Robert's enterprise was taken over John Brogden and Sons of Lancashire. John Brogden sent his 22 year old son James to run the Tondu business and the next ten years saw a major expansion. James rebuilt Tondu House and ran the 1,100 acre farm as well as the iron works. He built Park Terrace to house his workers, reopened the Tywith mine and opened others at Park Slip in Aberkenfig, Garth in Maesteg and the Tynewydd and Wyndham collieries in the Ogmore

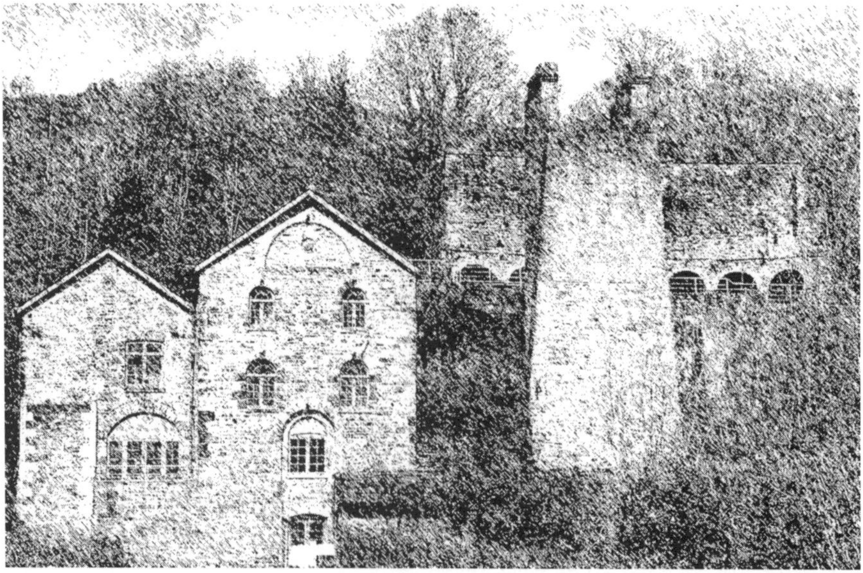

Tondu Ironworks

Valley. The Brogdens also built a school and built a railway from the Ogmore Valley to Tondu, also taking over the Llynfi to Porthcawl line and converting it from Brunel's seven foot broad gauge to the standard. A new port was built at Porthcawl.

At this time the ironworks flourished and there were coke ovens on the ironworks site and south of the Cribwr Colliery.

Old maps also show that Tondu had its own brewery in the 1870s, situated near the Wesleyan Chapel.

In addition to the railways, there were a number of tramways, one of which ran from Park Terrace to the Bridgend Branch line which was still in operation in the early 1950s, running underneath both Maesteg Road and Bryn Road.

Tondu became a hub for the railways with the three valley lines from the Ogmore, Garw and Llynfi connecting with lines to Porthcawl and Bridgend and to Llanharan and via the Ogwr Fach Valley to Tonyrefail and the Rhondda Valley.

In 1869 John Brogden died and Alexander Brogden moved to Tondu to take over the Glamorgan business. He lived at Coytrahen House. In 1872 he formed a new company, the Llynvi, Tondu and Ogmore Coal and Iron Company Limited, but the iron industry went into decline and the company went into liquidation.

Brogdens' empire was eventually taken over by North's Navigation Collieries (1889) Ltd owned by Colonel North who had made his money in the nitrate mines of Argentina. North with his manager, John Boyd Harvey, modernised the iron works. Harvey resided at Tondu house, as did subsequent managers until 1940. Iron making ceased in 1895, but Tondu remained the headquarters of North's Navigation Collieries until they were taken over by the National Coal Board in 1947. It also became a wagon repair works. In the same year British Railways took over the rail network which by then was part of the Great Western Railway.

Tondu House was taken over by the Ministry of Supply for the Pyrotechnic Research Department (PRD), linked to the Royal Ordnance Factory at Bridgend. Tondu House was demolished in 1963, but evidence of the experimental pyrotechnic work remains in the form of an observation bunker in the woods.

Around 1900, the Tondu Brickworks was established. It was sometimes known as the Evanstown works, though the bricks were clearly stamped Tondu. These works continued until 1974 and were demolished in 1977. The site, together with the old school site is now a retail and industrial park with a housing estate.

The Beeching era saw the end of passenger rail traffic at Tondu though this has since been partially revived with the Maesteg to Bridgend line.

Since the NCB gave up the Tondu site, the old iron works has been recognized as being of major historical importance as the most complete example of a Victorian iron works and Parc Tondu combines the remains of the works with nature trails and a BMX track. On Derllwyn Road is the Foxtroy residential home, formerly the iron works company's truck shop where workers would exchange tokens they had received in lieu of pay for goods at high prices.

West of the village, alongside the road which ran to Margam, was the Tondu Racecourse, used until the 1960s for 'flapper' or unregulated races, normally of ponies, which were subject to various betting scams.

The only remaining place of worship is the Wesleyan Methodist Chapel built in 1868 with its integral tower.

Tondu today is largely commuter territory with some local industry. There has been some modern housing development around the old brickworks site and the iron works. The Llynfi Arms, the only pub in the village, has closed.

One of the area managers for the National Coal board at Tondu was William Cleaver, better known as Billy Cleaver or 'Billy the Kick' who played international rugby at fly half for Wales and full back for the Lions between 1947 and 1950.

Tonmawr *Great Unploughed Land*

Tonmawr is a former mining village at the junction of the Pelenna and Gwenffrwd valleys four miles east of Neath. The village is in two parts with the old village of 19th and early 20th century properties now joined by modern houses taking advantage of he views offered across the Afan valley. The other part of the village is a 1950s and 60s housing estate. There is a village shop and post office, primary school and fitness centre. The area is being developed for tourism and the

Pelenna Mountain Centre south of the village is now a lodge linked to the Youth Hostel Scheme offering self catering accommodation in lodges together with an on site restaurant.

The area offers walking and mountain biking through beautiful forest scenery.

Tonmawr was reached by the South Wales Mineral Railway on the route between Briton Ferry and Glyncorrwg in 1861. In 1902 there was an accident on the line above Tonmawr. The line from Tonmawr to Glyncorrwg was single line and trains would pass at Cymer. On this occasion the 4.30 afternoon train from Glyncorrwg was carrying a Mr Perrot, a cashier of the colliery, in the engine, together with seven others in the guards van. The railway was not authorized to carry passengers but it had been the practice to allow residents to travel in empty trucks or the guard's van because of the remoteness of the village. Mr Perrot asked that the trains pass at Tonmawr to save time on his journey. Unfortunately the up-train had already left when the message was sent. An attempt was made to contact the signal box at Tonmawr but the signalman had left early. The result was a head on collision in the tunnel above Tonmawr with two of the passengers killed and others injured.

Industry came early to this mountainous village with a peat and charcoal production facility above the valley of the Nant Blaenpelenna. The Welsh Freehold Colliery appears to have been the first major mining operation at Tonmawr, opening possibly as early as the 1830s. There are the remains of a colliery ventilation furnace tower erected to provide air to the mine. Over the years it was known as the Mercantile, Blaenmawr and the Garth Colliery and employed over 200 men. It closed in 1964. The North End Colliery opened in 1911, employing around 80 miners . It closed in the 1930s. Merthyr Llantwit Colliery in the Gwenffrwd valley opened in 1898. Employing up to 205 men it closed in 1926. The Whitworth Colliery again in the Gwenffrwd valley was under German ownership. Digging started in 1907 but the coal was much deeper than anticipated and although some 170 men were employed in sinking the pit between 1907 and 1911, no coal was ever produced and the mine was abandoned.

Bethel Methodist Chapel was built in 1907 but has been replaced by a house. There is a modern wooden mission church set in a colourful garden.

Tonna *Unploughed Lands*

Tonna is a large village to the north of Neath lying along the eastern side of the River Neath and the Neath Canal, opposite Aberdulais. In 1884 the village consisted of Tonnau House, a few houses and a chapel. It takes its name from the Welsh Tonnau meaning 'grassland' and despite massive expansion throughout the 20th century retains a green feel.

The village has a hospital, primary school, a number of pubs and a mini supermarket. There is the modern Noddfa Newydd Baptist Church, Nazareth Calvinistic Methodist Chapel, built in 1862 and rebuilt in 1880.

The imposing neo-Gothic St Anne's church was built in 1893 in cruciform style with a chancel apse and entrance through the north tower, topped by a spire positioned just west of the north transept. It underwent a refurbishment, completed in 2013. St Anne's Church Hall is now a Sunni Islamic Centre.

Above the village on Fairyland Road is the Ivy Tower, built by the Mackworth family in the 1740s as a ballroom. Now a ruin, it remains a landmark in the valley and is Grade II Listed.

In 1839 the Glyncorrwg Mineral Railway, known as Parsons' Folly was started, an eight mile tramway connecting the Blaencregan coal deposits to the Neath Canal at Tonna. Completed in 1842 the track had been lifted by 1852 but its course can be traced.

Adjacent to the former railway on Cefn Morfydd are two cairns believed to be Bronze Age and the earthwork of an enclosure which appears to be associated with the cairns.

On Blaen Cwm, to the east of the village on the track which continues from the end of Fairyland Road are the earthworks of a Roman marching camp. Contained within the camp are the earthworks of a defended enclosure while to the east are the remains of a Bronze Age cairn.

Trebanos *High Placed Dwellings*

Trebanos is a village on the B4603 road from Clydach to Pontardawe in the Swansea valley.

The village was industrial in origin, with the Pheasant Bush Tinplate Works built in 1835 by William Parsons above the ninth lock of the

Swansea Canal. The site of the works was just north of the rugby ground and the canal at this point is intact.

Coal mining was carried on in the village until 1964 when the Daren Colliery, situated above Lloyd Road closed. It opened in 1906 and operated under various companies employing up to 180 men.

Housing in the village is mainly 19th or early 20th century with some modern housing. There are a few shops, a post office, takeaway restaurants, service station, primary school, Trebanos Rugby Club and the Colliers Arms.

Trebanos Tabernacle Methodist Chapel was built in 1842 above Swansea Road near Glyn-Meirch Road. The graveyard remains but the chapel has been demolished. Graig Unitarian Chapel was built in 1893 at the junction with Graig Road. Gosen Independent Chapel was built 1865, modified 1869 and rebuilt 1891. St Michael and All Angels church was built in 1912 as a mission church with the architect G. T. Bassett of Aberystwyth. The church consists of a nave, chancel, vestry, north porch and western bellcote. The east window dates from 1912 while other stained glass windows are by Celtic Studios of the 1950s.

Tythegston

Tythegston is a small village situated just off the A4106 road to Porthcawl. The original Welsh name was Llandudwg after St Tudwg's church and the English name seems to have been derived from this, being shown over the years as Tedegstowe (1260) Tegestowe (1332) Tythestowe (1429 and Tythegston (1525). That there was a settlement here prior to the Norman invasion is shown by the dedication to St Tudwg an early Welsh saint from the Gower where he was a pupil of St Cennydd.

Following the Norman appropriation of Glamorgan, Tythegston became part of the demesne lordship of Newcastle and the church became a chapel attached to Tewkesbury Abbey in 1173. The present building dates from the 14th century but was rebuilt in 1876 by the architect John Prichard. The chancel appears to be a weeping chancel, slightly out of line with the nave. This was thought to be a representation of Christ's head leaning to one side on the cross, but is more likely due to the builders taking their east compass point from sunrise on Easter Day in different years as the chancel was normally a later addition. The church which consists of a nave, chancel, western bellcote and south porch is now used as a business unit.

Tythegston Court on the A4106 is a nine bedroom house with extensive grounds advertised for rent in 2012 at £5,000 a month. The Court is thought to have been built originally as a fortified house by the Turbervilles in the early 14th century. Wilcock Turberville the illegitimate son of Richard Turberville was granted the manor of Tythegston by his legitimate brother Payn in 1300. The Court remained in the family through to 1533 and Parliamentary records show that there was once a tower at the Court. In 1438 Lady Margaret Malefant was forced into a marriage with Lewis Leyshon in the tower and subsequently sought redress through Parliament.

Tythegston Court passed through marriage to the Loughor family who converted the medieval house into a Tudor manor house. In 1708 the estate passed by marriage to the Knight family who carried out extensive alterations 1765-72 and 1810.

Fenton reported that there was a well known as Ffynnon Ivan, "presumed to cure the King's Evil" otherwise known as scrofula, a tuberculous infection of the lymph nodes in the neck.

There has been some recent development of two houses at Lower Farm behind the church, but the village remains small.

In 1619 Court records show that John David, of Tythegston, was indicted "for cutting or gelding the privie members of John Wm a chield of abouts xen yeere oulde."

Upper Killay

Upper Killay is a gateway to Gower from the east. The main road through the village passes over a cattle grid to the west, marking the start of Fairwood Common. In the 19th century the village consisted of a few farm workers' cottages. There was an increase in the early part of the 20th century as industry grew in the surrounding areas. Fairfield Common airfield was developed by the RAF in 1940 and this saw a further growth in population which has continued with Upper Killay now a commuter village. Houses tend to be well spaced with large gardens, no doubt ripe for infill. There is a village Hall with playing fields and the old village pond is now a wildlife habitat. The village has a sports and leisure store as well as a village shop. Providence Congregational Chapel was built in 1807 and rebuilt in 1911. It is now known as the Pines Congregational Church.

Waunarlwydd *The Lord's Heath*

Waunarlwydd is a village six miles north-west of Swansea. The village name dates from the medieval period, when it belonged to the Lords of Gower. By the 19th century the land was in the ownership of the Stepney family the last of whom was Lady Catherine Meriel Stepney who died in 1952.

The 19th century saw the village develop as a mining community with a number of small mines in the vicinity. Further development occurred during the Second World War when a munitions factory was built to the north of the village. This became the Alcoa factory which closed in 2007.

Waunarlwydd stands on a ridge with the valley of the Afon Llan to the north and Cwmlloyd Wood Nature Reserve to the south. There were two major streets along the ridge, Swansea Road and Victoria Road, where the older houses of the village are built. Since the 1950s the village has expanded and now has a supermarket and mini market, takeaway restaurants, two primary schools and the Masons Arms, the Farmers Arms and the Grill House Restaurant.

A mission church was built in 1887, later becoming St Barnabas parish church. It has a nave, chancel, north porch and western bellcote.

Sardis Independent Chapel was built in 1852 and rebuilt in 1859, and 1909. It is now a private dwelling. Bethany English Baptist Chapel was built in 1876 and rebuilt in 1908. Zion Welsh Baptist Chapel was built in 1872, and rebuilt in 1895. Now known as Seion, it is in need of repair, but is still open.

Wernffrwd *Alder Stream*

Wernffrwd is a hamlet on the north Gower coast between Crofty and Llanrhidian. Development has taken place to the north of the main road and along Marsh Road , taking advantage of the views across the marsh and the estuary. On Marsh Road is the little single cell mission church of St David.

West Cross

West Cross is a 1960s housing estate built between Mayals and Norton to the north of Oystermouth. There is a mixture of housing and two schools. There is a parade of shops on the sea front including a supermarket and post office.

Bethany Baptist Chapel was built in 1850.

Wyndham

Wyndham is a small former mining village on the western side of the Ogmore Valley, above Ogmore Vale. Just to the north was the site of the Wyndham Colliery, established in 1868 by John Brogden. Village and Colliery are named after the Wyndham family which owned Dunraven Castle and its estates from 1642. Ownership of the mine later passed to North Navigation and then to Cory Brothers who operated the mine until 1947. The colliery continued in production until 1983 and was the last major colliery in the valley to close. It employed up to 1,300 men and after 1957 was linked underground to the Western Colliery in Nantymoel. There is a memorial in a field some 550 yards north of the Wyndham Arms.

The village was the site of Ogmore Grammar School, which stood between Coronation Street and Fairy Glen. Established in 1910 it closed in 1977. The area has since been used for housing.

St David's Church was opened in 1879, initially consisting of a nave and porch, the chancel, sanctuary and vestry were added in 1884.

The Wyndham Arms was one of the early buildings in the village, built as part of a terrace before 1877. The village has a mini supermarket.

The area has been landscaped and apart from the housing and the Aber Field sports ground, built between Wyndham and Pricetown, has largely been returned to its pre 1865 condition.

Ystalyfera

Ystalyfera is a village in the Swansea Valley four miles north-east of Pontardawe, at the confluence of the Tawe and Twrch rivers.

The name is derived from Ynys Tal y Veran, meaning the end of a shared river meadow.

Industry came to Ystalyfera in 1838 when James Palmer Budd established a furnace in the village. By 1863 it was the home to the largest iron and tinplate works in the world. The introduction of steel saw the decline of the iron works and following Budd's death in 1880 the works closed in 1885.

Commercial coal mining started in 1812 when the Pwllbach Colliery was sunk by Daniel Harper. It was mined intermittently until 1893 when it was owned by D. W. Davis. It increased production and employment, with 28 men employed in 1893 rising as high as 500 before the colliery was closed in 1966. Tirbach Slant Colliery was opened in 1898 and at its peak in 1936 employed 651 men before closing in 1940.

The village today has little industry and is a commuter village for Swansea and Neath. It is built on the west bank of the River Tawe and is by-passed by the Swansea to Brecon road. There is a good range of shops with a two mini supermarkets. Pubs appear to have survived with the Old Swan, the New Swan Hotel and the Corner House and there is a coffee bar restaurant. There are two primary schools.

Ystalyfera was in the parish of Llanguicke until 1903 when it became a parish in its own right. Holy Trinity church was built in 1844 at a cost of £500 at the southern end of the village. It was enlarged in 1862 and continued until 1987 when it was condemned as being structurally unsound and demolished in 1988. The outline of this cruciform church is retained in a memorial garden in the graveyard.

The church of St David was built in 1888-91 with the architects J. B. Wilson, Glendinning Moxham and M. B. Adams. The church, built on a north-east south-west axis, has a nave, chancel, a south-east transept and a north-west vestry. The unusual circular tower with spire is off the vestry.

The first chapel in the village was Tant-teg Congregational Chapel, built in 1821 and rebuilt in 1841 and 1865. A landslip in 2012 left the future of the chapel in doubt. The English Congregational Church was built on Commercial Street in 1871 with an imposing rose window and tower topped with a spire in Gothic style. It was demolished in 2005. Caersalem Baptist Chapel was formed in 1854 with 40 members and the chapel was officially opened in 1858. Jerusalem Calvinistic Methodist Chapel was built in 1857 and rebuilt in 1881 and is still in use, as is Wern Independent Chapel, built in 1864. Zoar Baptist Chapel was built in 1847 and rebuilt in 1858, 1867 and 1899. It has now been demolished. Capel Seion, Wesleyan Methodist Chapel was built in 1861 and has now been replaced by a modern bungalow. Gurnos Road Chapel was built in 1840 as a Wesleyan Methodist Chapel. It was subsequently sold to the Congregationalists in 1858 and rebuilt in 1914.

Ynysforgan *Morgan's River Meadow*

Ynysforgan is a village immediately north of Junction 45 of the M4, to which it gives its name. Originally a ribbon development along the road to Ynystawe and Clydach, it has expanded to the west since the 1960s with new housing developments. There are no places of worship or shops in the village but there is a primary school.

Ynystawe *Tawe River Meadow*

Ynystawe is a ribbon development along the B4603 north of Junction 45 of the M4 on the road to Clydach. The village runs along the western bank of the River Tawe and recent years have seen the village develop to the west with houses enjoying views over the Swansea valley.

In the14th and early 15th century it was the home of Hopcyn ap Tomos who brought together much of the Welsh literature of the time, including the *Mabinogion* into the *Red Book of Hergest*, now housed in the Bodleian Library at Oxford. During its life the manuscript of 362 pages passed from Hopcyn's family to the Vaughans of Tretower in Breconshire, then to the Mansels of Margam and somehow it found its way into the possession of Revd Thomas Wilkins whose son donated it to Jesus College Oxford the current owners. Hopcyn was regarded as an expert on bardic lore and was consulted by Owain

Glyndwr as to the bardic prophecies about his fate. There is a memorial in Ynystawe Park.

There is an industrial estate to the north of the village and a primary school, but there is no shop in the village though there is the Millers Arms, no doubt in recognition of Ynys Tawe flour mill, built in 1810 by Edward Martin. The mill used the run off water from the Swansea Canal to power the waterwheel. The mill was situated to the east of Moriah Baptist Chapel, built in 1892.

Sources and further reading

Bibliography

Barber J. T. *A Tour throughout South Wales and Monmouthshire* , 803
Baring-Gould, Sabine *A Book of South Wales,* 1905
Baring-Gould, Sabine and Fisher, John *The Lives of the British Saints,* 1907
Cambrensis, Geraldus *The Itinerary Through Wales of Archbishop Baldwin (1188),* 1908 Translation
Carlisle, Nicholas *A Topographical Dictionary Of The Dominion Of Wales,* 1811
Cliffe, Charles Frederick *The Book of South Wales,* 1848
Evans C. J. *History of Llangynwyd Parish,* 1887
Evans C. J. *The Story of Glamorgan,* 1908
Fenton, Richard *Tours in Wales (1804-1813),* 1917
Leigh, Samuel *Leigh's Guide to Wales & Monmouthshire,* 1839
Lewis, Samuel *A Topographical Dictionary of Wales,* 1833 and 1845
Malkin, Benjamin H. *The Scenery Antiquities and Biography of South Wales,* 1807
Morgan, Thomas *The Place Names of Wales,* 1912
Nicholas, Thomas *The History and Antiquities of Glamorgan,* 1874
Rees, Thomas *The Beauties of England and Wales South Wales,* 1815
Roscoe, Thomas and Meredith, Charles *Wanderings and Excursions in South Wales,* 1844
Rowlands, John *Historical Notes of the Counties of Glamorgan Carmarthen and Cardigan,* 1866
Sikes, Wirt *British Goblins,* 1880
Wilkins, Charles *Tales and Sketches of Wales,* 1879

Online resources

Coflein
http://www.castlewales.com
www.enjoygower.com
www.genuki.org.uk
www.welshcoalmines.co.uk